BRONZE AGE WARFARE

BRONZE AGE WARFARE

Richard Osgood and Sarah Monks
with Judith Toms

SUTTON PUBLISHING

First published in the United Kingdom in 2000 by
Sutton Publishing Limited · Phoenix Mill
Thrupp · Stroud · Gloucestershire · GL5 2BU

British Library Cataloguing in Publication Data
A catalogue record for this book is available from the British Library.

ISBN 0-7509-2363-6

Typeset in 10/12 pt Sabon.
Typesetting and origination by
Sutton Publishing Limited.
Printed and bound in England by
J.H. Haynes & Co. Ltd, Sparkford.

CONTENTS

List of Illustrations

PREFACE

The original idea for this book was conceived by Richard Osgood following the completion of his thesis in 1996, subsequently published as *Warfare in the Late Bronze Age of North Europe*. He is responsible for writing Chapters Two and Four on north-western and central Europe respectively. He is currently involved in a number of field projects in northern Europe, including excavations of the Bronze Age linear ditch and human burials at Tormarton in south Gloucestershire.

The contributions of Sarah Monks and Judith Toms, who both have significant research interests in the Bronze Age, gave the project a more pan-European approach and allowed a broader range of evidence to be studied and evaluated.

Sarah Monks, who has co-written the book and is responsible for writing Chapters Three and Six, has been carrying out research on warfare in the West Mediterranean, and specifically Spain, for the past five years. Her thesis 'The role of conflict and competition in the development of prehistoric West Mediterranean societies from the late 4th to early 2nd millennium BC' was completed in 1998. Her research interests have focused largely on Copper and Bronze Age societies in many different parts of the Mediterranean, though specifically within Iberia, Cyprus and the Aegean.

Judith Toms has written Chapter Five on the Italian Bronze Age, and has given advice on the book as a whole. Her main area of research is the proto-history of Italy, and she has studied in particular Villanovan cemeteries and the symbolic nature of material culture in Villanovan and early Etruscan contexts.

The authors are grateful to the following people and organisations for their help and advice in bringing this book to fruition. Richard Osgood would like to thank Professors Richard Bradley, Anthony Harding, Barry Cunliffe and John Evans; Simon Pressey, Alison Wilkins and Kenton White for a number of the illustrations; Ian Cartwright for several of the photographs and Dr Mike Parker-Pearson who originally suggested that he should take a further look at Tormarton. Sarah Monks would like to thank Professors Richard Bradley and Robert Chapman; Dr Sturt Manning; David Mason (for some great photos); Simon Pressey (for the reconstruction drawing); Eva Baboula and Gerry Cox. Judith Toms would like to thank Doctors A. Sherratt, S. Sherratt, J. Robb, E. Macnamara, S. Swaddling and L. Vagnetti. Illustrations not otherwise credited are the work of the authors.

In addition, we wish to thank all the museums, institutions and individuals that granted us permission to use many of the photographs in this book. Finally, our thanks go to Rupert Harding and Sarah Cook of Suttons for their patience and perseverance.

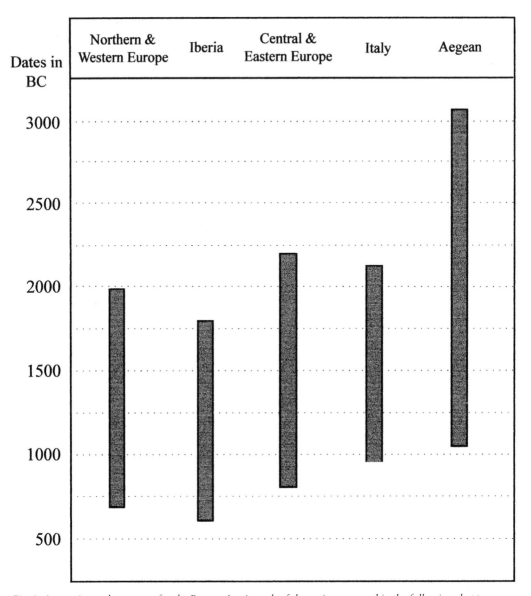

Fig. 1. Approximate date ranges for the Bronze Age in each of the regions covered in the following chapters.

ONE

INTRODUCTION

There has been a recent rise in the popularity of archaeological studies of warfare, although most of these have focused on a particular regional area or on specific case studies. Much of this work has been undertaken on the Roman or medieval periods where we have good documentary evidence to aid the interpretation of warfare, warriors and weapons. Prehistoric warfare has generally been treated with greater caution and many believe the evidence is too unreliable, uneven and open to many different interpretations. There has also been a tendency, when referring to the prehistoric period, to use ethnographic analogies to 'fill in the gaps' where evidence is patchy or difficult to interpret. Although the use of ethnographic case studies makes an important contribution to the study of archaeology, this present study tries to avoid the use of cross-cultural analogies between the prehistoric data and information on warfare from more recent societies.

A few recent publications have been significant in raising the 'profile' of prehistoric warfare, including *Ancient Warfare* (John Carman & Anthony Harding, eds), *Material Harm* (John Carman, ed.), *War before Civilization* (Lawrence Keeley), *Warfare in the Late Bronze Age of North Europe* (Richard Osgood) and *Troubled Times: Violence and Warfare in the Past* (Debra Martin & David Frayer, eds). In addition, there have been a number of articles in journals, although these typically focus on particular regional areas or specific cultural groups, or on types of analysis, for example, use-wear studies on weapons, skeletal studies or interpretations of rock art.

So where does this book fit in? It is intended to provide a general approach to warfare in Europe, addressing many of the key issues within warfare studies on a broad scale. The various chapters are specific to particular regions, and are written by people with a keen research interest in those areas, and within each chapter a multi-disciplinary approach is adopted, discussing a range of different types of evidence to produce a more rounded picture of the nature and frequency of combat, the weapons and armour employed, and the role of warfare in society, seen through burials and artistic traditions. The aim is not to provide a complete review of all the evidence, interpretations and theories on the data, because each region would then require a book of its own, but rather to identify general patterns and trends in the evidence for warfare and cite specific examples where appropriate. Of course, the period defined (and dated) as the 'Bronze Age' differs from region to region, a matter that is raised and discussed in each chapter. None the less, a cogent argument as to the essence of conflict in the Bronze Age of Europe can be produced.

Each chapter begins with a brief look at the preceding Copper Age or Neolithic period as a way of introducing the evidence for the Bronze Age. This is followed by a study of the various strands of evidence for warfare: settlement patterns, fortifications, burial and skeletal evidence, weapons and body protection, art and iconography. In terms of settlement patterns and fortifications, we consider what types of site were being occupied and the evidence for natural and artificial defences, and look at how the fortified, hilltop and non-fortified sites relate to one another in terms of their location, inter-visibility, function and so on. We cite examples of fortified sites, describing the nature of their defences and their development through time, including phases of destruction, repair and elaboration. The question of whether the defences were purely functional, or whether they served other social or symbolic purposes, is assessed.

We then move from the settlement sites to the people that lived in them (or at least to their physical remains). The skeletons of Bronze Age people provide perhaps the most unequivocal evidence for violence in the shape of injuries, many of them fatal. However, it is often difficult to distinguish between injuries caused by accidents and those sustained during fighting, and only a small number of examples of injuries and deaths from the Bronze Age can be conclusively attributed to violent actions. Death in combat need not leave any trace of trauma on the bones for the palaeopathologist to examine. In addition, a skeleton bearing, say, clear cut-marks on the bones may actually represent the physical manifestation of the result of a judicial execution, a murder or perhaps even post-mortem ritual treatment, as opposed to combat. Bearing this in mind, inferences are drawn from those skeletons which do seem to be reliable indicators of injuries through violence. The inferences made from this evidence relate to the method of violence used, weapon types, the angle and intensity of the assault (tactics), the types of injuries sustained and the likelihood of survival. The skeletal evidence is also considered within the context of the burial record as a whole in order to isolate unusual burial practices which may be significant. The so-called 'warrior graves' of the Bronze Age, typically accompanied by a rich array of weapons and warrior paraphernalia, are also discussed.

The evidence for weapons and body protection comes largely from burials, and thus not from the original context of use. Although some weapons may have been made purely for deposition in rich graves as votive offerings, or perhaps for ceremonial use, others were clearly damaged during combat and were repaired or recycled. Furthermore, it is clear that weapons were sometimes deliberately damaged in a more votive manner – for example, the ritual destruction or 'killing' of Late Bronze Age swords that were then deposited in water, or the deliberate stabbing of the shield from South Cadbury in Somerset. Though these blows were not received in combat, the votive damage may still have been connected to combat, perhaps being administered to destroy any items that symbolised the enemy.

A further problem with weapons is their multi-functionality. Whereas swords were clearly used for fighting (and ritual battles), knives, daggers, sticks, stones, arrows and spears could have been used for other purposes, such as for hunting or as tools. In addition, we must assume that only a relatively small percentage of the actual weapons used have been preserved in the archaeological record. We know from areas where good preservation occurs and also from the ethnographic record that weapons and armour were frequently made from perishable materials, such as leather and wood. Fortunately in some areas of Europe there is relatively good preservation of these perishable materials (*see* Chapter Two), while rock carvings and cave paintings indicate the types of evidence that might be missing from the archaeological record. Again, caution must be applied in always interpreting these as functional items, rather than as exaggerated symbols of power or status, or as objects used ritually rather than practically. For the prehistoric period there is much that we do not know, and in the absence of written records much that we will never know, such as the motives or causes of violence, attitudes to fighting, and its impact on society, the economy and political structure – these must be interpreted from the evidence available. For the Aegean we do have some written records, Linear B tablets, which aid our interpretation of warfare in that region, although they do not provide all the answers (*see* Chapter Six).

Throughout this work care has been taken not to assume that those involved in warfare had to be male. There are certainly documented examples from later periods of women taking an active part in combat, be it in the French Revolution, the Boudican revolt or the Vietnam conflict. Famously, the women of the Teutonic tribe, the Ambrones, fought not only the Roman General Marius in the second century BC, but also attacked their men-folk for retreating from the Romans. In addition, graves assumed to be of males simply because of the assemblages of weaponry they contain, may in fact be of females. This is the case with numerous examples from the Anglo-Saxon period and there are also examples from Iron Age Russia and possibly from Beaker burials in Britain. Women had an important role to play – either as active combatants, as victims or objects/causes of war, or in the pre- and post-war preparations and celebrations – and this should be borne in mind.

The archaeological evidence is inevitably very static and does not paint a very dynamic picture of warfare. Fortunately a range of paintings, engravings and carvings have been preserved, some of which depict scenes of war while others bring us face-to-face with Bronze Age warriors. Although these depictions are open to a range of different interpretations (as discussed in each chapter), they form an important category of evidence for the study of warfare. They help us to reconstruct different forms of fighting and to understand how weapons were used and what types of body protection were worn, and in some cases it even becomes possible to speculate on the identity of the combatants. At the end of each chapter we put forward an interpretation of what the evidence as a whole infers about motives and causes, defensive and offensive tactics, and attitudes to warfare and warriors (both living and in death), set within the context of Bronze Age communities as a whole.

By studying a specific period in time across a wide geographical area, we are able to make inter-regional comparisons and begin to suggest reasons for the existence of similarities and differences. This enables us to compare different interpretations and theories while continually reassessing our ideas and preconceptions of what we think warfare was like in the past. The evidence presented for each regional area is then summarised in the final chapter, with a review of general trends in warfare across Europe as a whole, touching on the types of fighting practised, the weapons used, the tactics and strategies employed (both defensive and offensive), the injuries sustained, and the role of warfare within society.

The overall aim of this book is to present a large body of evidence in an accessible and readable way, and to summarise information from different countries which is otherwise available only in native languages and in specialist or obscure publications. Further reading is suggested at the end of each chapter – we have tried to restrict this to literature which is both in English and easily available. A more detailed bibliography is provided at the end and a glossary of terms used in the book is also given. Obviously there are many problems surrounding the detection of evidence for warfare in the archaeological record, but when all the different strands of evidence are drawn together it is possible to weave a picture of the warfare that undoubtedly took place in Bronze Age Europe. As the following chapters demonstrate, there is much that we do not know about warfare in the Bronze Age, but clearly much can be gleaned from the archaeological record.

DEFINING WARFARE

It would be sensible at this point to undertake a brief examination of what is meant by warfare and to define some elements of terminology – for example, how is warfare to be differentiated from skirmishes, raids, revenge killings and so forth?

War is viewed by historians as organised, strategically planned, militarily disciplined and expressing political policy. Clausewitz, a veteran of the Napoleonic Wars, saw it as the continuation of 'political intercourse', but presupposed that it could be strictly defined, taking a number of distinct forms, and that it had a beginning and an end – i.e. war was an event rather than a part of everyday life. His work *On War* is perhaps the most famous book on the subject, although his ideas were coloured by modern perceptions of war and first-hand experience, and he gave no consideration to pre- or non-state forms of warfare which involved no distinction between the lawful and unlawful bearing of arms, a feature that pervaded much of the prehistoric period.

Clausewitz's work typifies one of the main problems surrounding the study of early forms of warfare, namely that military history, and therefore the literate world, has been dominated by 'civilised' warfare. The lack of publications on prehistoric warfare, coupled with modern concepts of war, created two main schools of thought during the seventeenth and eighteenth centuries. The first approach was expressed by Thomas Hobbes, a prominent English philosopher of the time, who regarded prehistoric people as primitive and violent, and their lives as 'solitary, poor, nasty, brutish and short'. A second approach put forward the view that civilised humans have fallen from a 'peaceful golden age'. Jean-Jacques Rousseau, a critic of Hobbes, was an early proponent of this theory. He argued that man was not naturally cruel and that violent behaviour among primitive societies, past and present, was inconsequential and rare (see Keeley 1996: 5–8; Monks 1997: 3–5). The problem with both these theories is that they interpret prehistoric warfare from an historical point of view, and both Hobbes and Rousseau based their theories on an eclectic range of ethnographic examples. Furthermore, the period of European expansion and the work of the early missionaries, which brought westerners into contact with more 'primitive' societies, seemed to confirm the picture painted by Hobbes, reaffirming the need for European pacification and the introduction of Christianity to bring order to these peoples.

In addition to the work of historians, anthropologists have also tried long and hard to find causes and explanations for different forms of warfare; this too has been problematic. Early accounts of primitive societies were heavily biased and often mis-recorded and ethnographers were often deprived of much information on many aspects of society, including the frequency of fighting and the different forms of warfare practised. This being said, it is now clear that, contrary to the views of Rousseau, very few societies were ever truly peaceful and warfare was a common phenomenon within the ethnographic record. It would seem that small, pre-state groups in particular found peace difficult to maintain and derived few benefits from it. In contrast, warfare, or the maintenance of a certain level of hostility, was seen as an important way of creating social relationships (whether peaceful or hostile), maintaining social dialogue between groups, and countering shortages and periods of risk. Therefore, it would appear that early man was not the peace-loving animal that Rousseau would have us believe.

Archaeologists have traditionally considered warfare to be a feature of complex societies and states, despite the notable absence of studies into early forms of warfare. 'The most widely used archaeological textbooks contain no references to warfare until the subject of urban civilizations is taken up' (Keeley 1996: 18), and therefore warfare is implied to be insignificant before this time. Where 'primitive' warfare is mentioned there is a great deal of eclecticism in the choice of ethnographic examples, many of which are inherently biased through the recording process. More often in archaeology, early forms of warfare are assumed or implied but rarely deemed worthy of detailed discussion. Conflict is all too often dismissed either as a natural human characteristic, requiring no explanation, or as the inevitable solution to some economic or environmental crisis or change (Monks 1997: 1). In response to the former, anthropologists turned to theories and arguments derived from biological and behavioural studies, focusing on the activities of non-human primates, and comparing and contrasting this with evidence derived from simple, pre-state societies, principally in the New World. However, the different forms of violence found within the majority of societies are too diverse and too complex to be explained simply in terms of natural aggression, or the need to kill. With regard to the second point, the inevitability of warfare among developing societies can by no means be taken for granted and the question of possible ecological/environmental/economic causes requires careful investigation.

Many of these arguments lack not only a discussion of early forms of warfare, but also neglect its evolution and development within a social setting, and include no detailed empirical evidence in support of these hypotheses. More than fifteen years ago Slavomil Vencl called attention to the lack of behaviourally oriented archaeological studies of warfare, and to the difficulties of recognising evidence for prehistoric conflict, leading to an over-emphasis on peaceful ancient Europeans (cited Milner 1995: 222). Yet he was simply reiterating what a handful of other scholars had already noted – the need for studies that traced the first instances and subsequent rise of warfare: in other words an evolutionary and empirical approach which would test whether warfare was inevitable among humans and, if not, what circumstances or conditions caused and perpetuated it. As we have already noted, one of the most common areas in which this problem arises is in using the concept of warfare as a factor in the development of state-level societies. Once again, theories on the development of states often incorporate some form of coercion or violence but they provide little discussion as to the development of warfare amid non-state and pre-state societies. Twenty years on such issues have still to be addressed in many areas of European and Mediterranean prehistoric archaeology.

TERMINOLOGY

Definitions of terms such as violence, aggression, conflict, war and warfare can be found in many anthropological texts. The fact that these terms are discussed in great detail in anthropology may account for their lack of definition within archaeology. Among archaeologists such terms are used freely, and often interchangeably, without recourse to subtle nuances of meaning. But, since these terms imply a great deal about the scale, form and intentionality of fighting, the context of their use should be carefully considered.

Violence and aggression are considered to be biological or behavioural traits which involve the use of force against others. These characteristics can relate to all scales of force, from disputes between individuals to intense warfare between organised groups, and can be more closely defined as 'harm-giving between human beings' through which a social advantage is secured over an opponent (Riches 1991: 282). Violence is the operation of harm-giving, whereas aggression can denote a whole range of social behaviours (ibid. pp. 284–5).

'War', on the other hand, suggests greater scale, organisation and political direction, and has modern connotations of organised military action comprising the use of force and negotiation, and dictated by policy. Such factors are not necessarily appropriate to a discussion of the prehistoric situation, and therefore we advocate the use of the term 'warfare'. Warfare is not necessarily premeditated, nor governed by specific policies or goals, and it may not involve large numbers of organised warriors, nor be the only means of achieving human goals. Warfare can refer to a hostile situation or to the regular occurrence of violence, or may even describe a type of lifestyle. It covers a much broader range of situations and actions, and most definitions make allowance for this: 'Warfare means all organised forms of inter-group homicide involving combat teams of two or more persons, [and] explicitly includes highly localised and small-scale incidents which would more usually be described as skirmishes, raids or feuds' (Divale & Harris 1976, cited Riches 1991: 290). Others have argued that to be distinguished as warfare, rather than as skirmishes or tussles, action must be purposeful: Warfare 'refers to purposeful violence calculated to advance the ambitions of separate political factions, regardless of who was involved, the regularity of fighting, the numbers of participants, or specific combat tactics' (Milner 1995: 221). In other words, violence or threats of an aggressive nature must have involved a motive or have been deliberate. Indeed, the threat of violence is certainly a major element of conflict and no casualties need be involved. To take a much more recent example, after the Falklands War of 1982 Britain and Argentina were still in a state of war for a number of years although no actual combat took place: here the very threat of warfare was important. Within an archaeological context the main problem is in determining the intentionality of violence and the decision-making process.

'Defence' is another term which is commonly brandished in archaeological discussions of warfare and its associated structural features. We talk about sites in terms of their natural defences or their defensible locations, and mention the presence of artificial defences, adding words like 'strategic' and 'tactical'. Defence has been defined by one archaeologist as 'any action that constitutes resistance against attack' (Rowlands 1972: 447) and it is argued that aggressive behaviour stimulates a cultural response which includes the construction of defences to protect whatever is being challenged, whether it be objects, people or a defined space. Defensive action is therefore geared towards repelling an enemy attack or threat, and often takes the form of constructing physical barriers. Other defensive measures include fleeing or forming alliances or other relationships which reduce the likelihood of an attack. The building of actual barriers is seen as the most common form of defence, perhaps because of their physical presence and often their longevity. However, there is no easy way to distinguish between what is and what is not a defensive structure, since this depends on a number of social and cultural factors. The most fundamental of these are the perceptions and intentions of the constructors. It seems that the definition of defence also involves territoriality through the definition of boundaries, ownership and the need to exclude humans or animals from certain spaces, probably achieved through some kind of force or preventive measure.

To us, 'warfare' implies some degree of organisation or purposeful planning, either in terms of weapon and armour production, the provision of defensive measures or the use of offensive strategies. Unorganised fighting is different; it is *ad hoc*, often opportunistic and sporadic, unplanned and often has no obvious or consistent motives. In addition, such combat also leaves few traces in the archaeological record. In the chapters which follow we will see that this often characterises the nature of warfare in the early prehistoric periods (Mesolithic, Neolithic and Copper Age), based on our knowledge and understanding of the evidence, but in the Bronze Age things begin to change. In this period we have more concrete evidence that defences were being erected for the protection of sites (often involving a significant investment of time, labour and materials), weapons were being produced specifically for fighting (as opposed to hunting, or hunting and fighting) and warriors were being provided with body protection. Furthermore, warfare and warriors were being ascribed social status through the elaboration of their weapons, armour and other accoutrements, and they were represented in art and commemorated in death.

One caveat that should be raised is that the increasingly ritual and social aspects of warfare greatly skews our understanding of Bronze Age warfare and it would be naïve not to allow for a symbolic as well as a functional interpretation for much of the evidence. For example, the introduction of the chariot could be argued to reflect the change to a more mobile form of fighting, but it is important to consider how feasible this would have been: was the terrain suitable for fighting from chariots? What weapons would have been used and how? What is the evidence for the use of horses? Were chariots largely ceremonial? How representative is the iconographic evidence and how can we reconcile the different interpretations of the depictions? Ethnographic case studies also reveal the more social and symbolic side of warfare in the form of mock battles, ritual fighting and ceremonial displays of weapons and warrior accoutrements. It is clear that these aspects of warfare may greatly alter our interpretation of practices of warfare in the past and we must be wary of always presenting a functional or practical interpretation of the evidence.

Furthermore, even taking into account any problems with the dataset, anthropology teaches us that imposing our modern perceptions of war and warfare on the past may also be wrong. Warfare is not necessarily something to be avoided whenever and wherever possible, something devastating and sporadic that breaks out during a continuum of peace. In many instances warfare could be argued to be a part of everyday life, a form of social interaction just like trade and exchange, marriage and feasting.

FURTHER READING

Carman, J. & Harding, A. 1999. *Ancient Warfare* (Sutton)

Carman, J. (ed.). 1997. *Material Harm* (Cruithne)

Clausewitz, C. von. 1968. *On War* (Penguin edn)

Haas, J. (ed.). 1990. *The Anthropology of War* (Cambridge)

Keeley, L.H. 1996. *War Before Civilization: the Myth of the Peaceful Savage* (Oxford)

Martin, D. & Frayer, M. (eds). 1997. *Troubled Times: Violence and Warfare in the Past* (War and Society vol. 3, Gordon & Breach)

Milner, G.R. 1995. 'An osteological perspective on prehistoric warfare', in L.A. Beck (ed.), *Regional Approaches to Mortuary Analysis* (Plenum Press), pp. 221–44

Monks, S.J. 1997. 'Conflict and competition in Spanish prehistory: the role of warfare in societal development from the late fourth to third millennium BC', *Journal of Mediterranean Archaeology* 10(1), pp. 3–32

Osgood, R. 1998. *Warfare in the Late Bronze Age of North Europe* (British Archaeological Reports Int. Series 694)

Riches, D. 1991. 'Aggression, war, violence: space/time and paradigm', *Man* 26, pp. 281–98

Rowlands, M.J. 1972. 'Defence: a factor in the organization of settlements', in P.J. Ucko, R. Tringham & G.W. Dimbleby (eds), *Man, Settlement and Urbanism* (Duckworth) pp. 447–62

TWO

NORTHERN AND WESTERN EUROPE

INTRODUCTION

For the purpose of this chapter, Northern and Western Europe is defined as Scandinavia, the Low Countries, France and the British Isles. Although often regarded as somewhat peripheral to the major areas of Bronze Age innovation (central Europe in particular), these areas were none the less of great importance. Not only were vital trade goods exported from the region, but major prestige goods for internal consumption were also produced.

Since the study of archaeology began, much work has been carried out on the possible chronological development of the Bronze Age throughout Europe. Broadly speaking, the current understanding of the progression of the Bronze Age in this region is as depicted in **Fig. 1** (*see* p. xii). The Low Countries are a little problematical as a precise chronology is still to be established, but this situation may well change as further radiocarbon dates are obtained. In general terms, however, it is unlikely to differ much from northern France.

Warfare was certainly not a new phenomenon in the Bronze Age of northern and western Europe: fortifications were constructed on sites of Neolithic age, famously at Crickley Hill in Gloucestershire, and a huge timber defensive structure was built at Mount Pleasant, Dorset (Mercer 1999). At Crickley Hill there even seemed to be possible evidence for an attack on the site with areas of burning and arrowheads scattered liberally around the defences.

In addition to the construction of defences, possible victims of combat from early prehistory have been found. Although, as we mentioned in the introduction, wounded individuals need not represent warfare at all, this remains one of the possible interpretations. France has possible Neolithic victims, including people killed by arrowheads from Aurignac, for example. Denmark provides an especially gruesome example of the potentially lethal nature of society in the shape of a body at Pormose. A bone projectile had pierced the nose of this individual, remaining in the skull, while another projectile had pierced the sternum, causing death (Bennike 1985: 110 and fig. 64). One of the bodies found within the chamber-tomb at Ascott-under-Wychwood in Oxfordshire had suffered an arrow wound, and the flint projectile was still embedded between the vertebrae. A further body from Britain, recovered from the Stepleton enclosure at Hambledon Hill in Dorset, also seems to have been struck down by an arrow (Mercer 1999: 154–6). Before the advent of metal, flint weapons, particularly arrows, seem to have been the main mode of killing both of animals for food and of humans in conflict.

There are numerous elements which, taken as a whole, provide a cogent, convincing argument for combat and conflict being a part of Bronze Age society. While not perhaps an everyday occurrence, warfare and raiding certainly played a part in people's lives across Europe. The Bronze Age has been described as the period of the first 'arms race', with weaponry being recovered from the archaeological record alongside other bronze goods. The apparent victims of these weapons and the defences constructed by societies to fend off attackers also lend support to the arguments for the existence of fighting. Such activity was depicted in the iconography of the Bronze Age and, although we do not have the written evidence available to scholars of the Aegean Bronze Age, these elements can hint at different types of combat.

SETTLEMENTS AND FORTIFICATIONS

Despite some regions of northern and western Europe being limited in archaeological evidence, it seems clear that from the start of the Bronze Age settlement was varied, with sites located on promontories, in marshes, in valleys, on hilltops and even in caves. New sites are still being excavated, which add to the overall understanding of the nature of settlement. What, though, can it add to the picture of warfare? From the early Bronze Age onwards, there appears to have been a degree of trade building up between societies consuming prestige goods over large distances. As we shall see later, such competition can lead societies into conflict. This in turn is perhaps reflected in the development of more defensive settlements and it is important to look at these types of Bronze Age settlement in detail.

Evidence for large-scale organisation of the landscape is perhaps best represented in south-west Britain, where Dartmoor has been much studied and provides a sizeable amount of useful information. Perhaps the best known Bronze Age settlement is Grimspound, which has a series of stone hut circles surrounded by an enclosure wall (**Fig. 2.1**). In addition, Merrivale has large and small stone hut circles near stone alignments. Shaugh Moor, again on Dartmoor, is similar to Grimspound and Merrivale, a number of circular stone buildings within an enclosure wall. This site, dating to around 1700–1600 BC, had both habitation areas and animal corrals. Large-scale organisation of the environment by the societies living there is beyond doubt, though by around 1200 BC, for whatever reason, most of these fields and settlements on Dartmoor were abandoned (Fleming 1988).

Dwellings in north and west Europe were not always round in shape. In the Low Countries, for example, we find long-houses. These can be over 20m long and have clearly demarcated zones within them for specially defined purposes – a region for livestock, another for human habitation. Such houses have been discovered at Elp, Drenthe and Zijderveld in southern Holland and at Fragtrup in Denmark. Long-houses seem to be heavily connected with agricultural practices, involving both crops and livestock (Coles & Harding 1979).

At Cannes-Écluse, France, there seems to be much evidence for craft production within the settlement, with metals and pottery being worked. Alongside this production there were a number of domestic dwellings, some of them quite substantial. Goods were also

Fig. 2.1. One of the Bronze Age stone huts at Grimspound, Dartmoor, England. The wall immediately behind this hut is the enclosing pound wall.

produced at Itford Hill, Sussex, and at other farmsteads in Britain (Parker-Pearson 1993). These settlements were thus not only farms, but were also concerned with the exchange of goods and materials. Although settlements were provided with enclosure fences, these seem to have been used for penning animals and demarcating space rather than for defence. Evidence for agricultural activities has been found in abundance on sites of the Early Bronze Age onwards, although large-scale archaeobotanical information is not found until the Middle Bronze Age. Farming seems to have been supplemented by the production of tradable goods on many sites as the Bronze Age progressed. Trade was also essential to the settlements of the later Bronze Age in Denmark. At Bulbjerg in Jutland pieces of amber were found in association with settlement and occupation debris which may perhaps indicate that the site was involved with the amber trade from the north through central Europe. At Hallunda in Sweden rectangular dwellings have been excavated which were of similar dimensions to the Elp long-houses. This site, positioned on a hill, seems to show evidence of metalworking in the form of crucibles and bronze rods.

In lowland Britain clusters of houses have been excavated at Blackpatch in Sussex and Trethellan Farm in Cornwall. These too had fences and evidence for agricultural production and storage. Blackpatch also produced loom-weights and a bronze razor along with pottery. In all of these examples, from the Early Bronze Age onwards, fences on lowland sites do not seem to have been established for defence against attack. Certainly there is little evidence from the early settlements for warfare or conflict.

However, hilltop sites were increasingly utilised, especially in the late Middle Bronze Age, with indications of the appearance of defensive fortifications and even, for want of a better word, hillforts. Increasingly, evidence is being found which places the origins of defended hilltop sites firmly in the Bronze Age, although in some cases defended hilltop sites of Neolithic date are known and may have been used in warfare. Hambledon Hill, Dorset, and Crickley Hill, Gloucestershire, are two examples. This is of huge importance

Fig. 2.2. Mam Tor hillfort, Derbyshire, England. This site had extensive defensive origins in the Bronze Age. (Photo: © Crown Copyright, NMR (D. Riley))

to our study, since the shift from settlement in open areas to hilltop sites with artificial fortifications seems to indicate pressures for defence.

Many of the best examples come from the British Isles, where a number of hilltop sites with enclosure ditches were established in the Middle Bronze Age, and some later had more substantial defences added, Norton Fitzwarren, Somerset, being a case in point. Here excavations recovered a Middle Bronze Age hoard and pottery in a trench pre-dating an Iron Age hillfort. The defences at Rams Hill in Berkshire consisted of an enclosure ditch and rampart. The ditch was steep-sided and flat-bottomed, ranging in width from 3 to 3.75m, and in depth from 0.9 to 1.24m. A series of radiocarbon dates obtained from samples taken at this site seem to indicate that the defences were constructed near the end of the Middle Bronze Age or early in the Late Bronze Age (Bradley & Ellison 1975).

Mam Tor in Derbyshire is one of the highest hillforts in Britain at around 509m OD (**Fig. 2.2**). The defences here enclose some 6.48ha, and although they post-date the Bronze Age there are certainly Middle Bronze Age elements, hinting at a possible Bronze Age precursor to the Iron Age site. A number of huts found in the interior yielded Bronze Age pottery and a Late Bronze Age socketed axe among other finds. This occupation material, together with radiocarbon dates spanning the period 1679–996 BC, led the excavators to postulate that this was an example of a *Höhensiedlung* (elevated settlement), with simple defences consisting of a palisade with ditches and banks added later.

By the Late Bronze Age fortification had become increasingly common. At Hog Cliff Hill near Maiden Newton, Dorset, a bank and ditch with timber defences was probably established in the Late Bronze Age/Iron Age transition. Though not on the scale of Rams Hill, for example, this site none the less shows the increasing tendency towards stronger fortifications. There are a number of substantial fortified sites in Yorkshire. Eston Nab, for example, had a couple of palisade trenches with Late Bronze Age pottery within them. Boltby Scar was equipped with ramparts and ditches which were also found to contain Bronze Age pottery. Thwing was a high-status settlement defended by substantial ramparts with a timber box-structure; Bronze Age pottery and bronze objects were recovered here. Certainly, the Late Bronze Age sees English fortification on a greater scale than earlier in the period (*see* Osgood 1998).

In Wales there is also evidence for hillforts. The first rampart at Dinorben in Clwyd consisted of layers of rubble or clay on rafts, revetted with a palisade. The rampart rested on an occupation layer which yielded a series of radiocarbon dates suggesting that the initial rampart was constructed at some time after the eleventh century BC, and possibly the ninth or eighth centuries BC. The Breiddin hillfort, Powys, yielded much Late Bronze Age occupation material, including weapons, tools, decorative objects, pottery and spindle-whorls. The defences at this site comprised a timber-framed box-rampart, the core of which consisted of stones ranging in size – from small boulders to large stones (Musson 1991). Radiocarbon dates again indicate that these defences were constructed in the Late Bronze Age. In general, box-ramparts and early hillforts in Britain occurred from the so-called Urnfield period onwards.

Irish hillforts, from Donegal to Wicklow, are now yielding radiocarbon dates of the Bronze Age. Charcoal samples from the rampart at Mooghaun fort, situated on a low hill overlooking the Shannon estuary in Co. Clare, gave a Late Bronze Age date of 1255–917 BC. A single date obviously does not allow us to make too many claims for the site, but it does add weight to the overall argument for hillforts emerging in significant numbers in the period. The trivallate hillfort at Haughey's Fort in Ulster has also yielded dates that are broadly contemporary with Mooghaun. The site of Dún Aonghasa, dramatically situated on a cliff edge on the Arran Islands, comprised a concentric series of walls, semi-circular in shape. Some of these appear to have Late Bronze Age elements. Finds of a clay spear and sword moulds were made. The site may have had important symbolic functions, particularly as it would have left any defenders with no retreat.

It was not just Britain that saw the development of hillforts in the Late Bronze Age. Many defended sites were already in existence in central and eastern Europe by this time (*see* Chapter Four). In addition, a series of hillforts was established in the Late Bronze Age in Sweden, Predikstolen near Uppsala being just one example. France, too, had a number of defended sites, Chateau-sur-Salins, Châtelet d'Etaules and Citu to name but three. These have in general been assigned later Urnfield (Ha B3) dates. The site at Châtelet d'Etaules was situated on a promontory around 12km north of Dijon, and enclosed around 7ha. This site had been fortified from the Neolithic onwards, but the first phase of Bronze Age occupation dates to around the tenth century BC. A box-structure of horizontal tree-trunks was built on the ruins of the earlier defences, and the centre then filled with stone to provide a formidable and very solid barrier. Surviving pieces of wood from this structure have produced a dendrochronological date of the tenth century BC. In the eighth century BC a number of 'arrow slots' were incorporated into the façade south of the rampart.

Hillforts become more prominent in the archaeological record at a time when the panoply of weaponry is becoming increasingly developed and more sophisticated. The defences at the sites mentioned above are of a size and morphology to suggest that, far from being constructed simply to reflect the power of the constructor(s) – prestige sites constructed for ritual or votive purposes – these fortified sites could certainly have fulfilled a functional defensive role.

Some lowland sites were also provided with artificial barriers by the end of the Bronze Age, and a number of these have been seen in the Low Countries and in Britain. The site at Springfield Lyons, Essex, boasted a 2m-deep ditch with a timber and earth rampart dating to *c*. 900 BC. Fascinatingly, in the ditch terminals on either side of the northern entrances to the site, the excavators found clay moulds possibly used for casting swords. This site may have been a farm or it may have had a more ritual purpose – as stated in Chapter One, not all barriers were for protection against attack. Lofts Farm, also in Essex, was another site enclosed with 'defences' that might not have helped in the event of an attack.

The late Middle Bronze Age in Britain saw a general division of the landscape, with long linear ditches being cut across substantial tracts of land, some of them persisting for many kilometres, such as the great Quarley Linear at Windy Dido, recently excavated by Barry Cunliffe (pers. comm.). In addition to these land divisions and the establishment of field systems in some places, we find all the aforementioned settlements with enclosure ditches and banks, and hilltop sites with more substantial defences across north and western Europe. To what end?

A number of explanations have been suggested for the construction of the later hilltop settlements: they were intended to protect trade routes; they were part of a network of settlements providing protection for the inhabitants of undefended sites; they were established as independent settlement units. Certainly the defended hilltop sites were vital to the protected river-based trade routes of central and eastern Europe. If raiding also occurred along rivers, then protection of these routes in the west would also have been vital. Hillforts in northern and western Europe are often found in locations that dominated land and riverine passes, suggesting that these trade routes were hugely significant. But the defended sites were not there simply for the protection of trade routes; they also played a role in the production of the trade goods. There is a large quantity of evidence for this in the form of spindle-whorls for the manufacture of woven goods, moulds or crucibles for metalworking, and other elements. Production of goods utilising static resources required static defences. In addition, there are defended sites that are seemingly connected to field systems, part of the general division of land, and reflecting heightened pressure on land for agricultural use. Hillforts were perhaps one response to an increasing threat to trade routes and goods, and to land. Once constructed, they would have necessitated a change in combat tactics.

What then of the smaller defended sites? One could perhaps make a case for a 'ritual' motive behind certain elements of construction, demarcating important spaces and routes of passage. Some sites may have been given banks and ditches to contain or keep out animals. In addition, some structures could have been established for pure bravado, and to reflect prestige upon the builder. However, the Late Bronze Age competition for land must have been equally significant on these lowland sites too, with people becoming less mobile than before, and some authors have suggested that food supplies were now being controlled in a more centralised fashion. Defences at these sites were created for similar reasons as the hilltop sites, and reflect increased raiding for land, food and/or prestige goods.

BURIALS AND PALAEOPATHOLOGY

'The greatnesse and numeroussnesse of the Barrows (the beds of Honour where now so many Heroes lie buried in Oblivion) doe speak plainly to us, that Death and Slaughter once rag'd here and there were the scenes, where terrible Battles were fought . . .'

John Aubrey, *Monumenta Britannica*

The famous British antiquarian John Aubrey believed that the round barrows so common in much of southern England were the products of warfare, and that those entombed within were warriors killed in battle. Much work has been done on the various methods Bronze Age societies employed to dispose of their dead, although this is beyond the remit of this book. However, it is important to provide a general indication of the changing funerary practices of the period and focus on certain specific examples. One cannot be too dogmatic in making statements about Bronze Age societies based solely on examining their methods of dealing with the dead. Any goods found with the remains of an individual were put there for a now-unclear purpose: were the grave-goods part of the equipment of the deceased or did they belong to his or her relatives or kin group; were they an expression of the ideals of the age or simply provided to assist the passage to the afterlife? By looking at certain sites within general trends it is possible to raise arguments about the nature of Bronze Age conflict. Within such an examination we can establish that weapons were an important part of the burial rites and thus were probably a significant element in Bronze Age societies.

Burials

In the later third millennium BC a particular assemblage of goods appeared in the burial record of the so-called 'Atlantic Zone' of Europe. Known as the Beaker package, it included weapons such as arrows, daggers and archers' wristguards, and a ceramic vessel called a Bell-Beaker owing to its shape when inverted (**Fig. 2.3**). Burials were found in tumuli, which often formed the focal points of later groups of round barrows, or were inserted into older monuments like the Neolithic West Kennett long barrow in Wiltshire. The archers of the age may have been clad in the sort of leather armour depicted in the carvings of Le Petit Chasseur in Switzerland (*see* Chapter Four), although no examples have yet been discovered in Beaker burials. Andrew Sherratt has suggested that these graves reflect the warrior symbolism so vital to this period of European prehistory (Sherratt, A.G.S., pers. comm.). The Bell-Beaker graves were an expression of the warrior values that were emerging as part of a more mobile and opportunistic way of life as the traditional social structures of the Neolithic broke down.

Fig. 2.3. The so-called Beaker package from a burial at Dorchester in England. Here the inhumation was accompanied by the beaker, an archer's wristguard and a bronze dagger. (Photo: Ashmolean Museum, Oxford)

Beakers and their associated burial goods are found along the Atlantic coasts, in Britain, Iberia and northern France, and even inland in the Rhineland and along rivers in central Europe. These were the trade-routes that were to be so vital as the Bronze Age progressed. It must not be assumed that all burials containing the Beaker package were of male individuals. Too often such burials have been sexed as male not from the skeletal material but from the grave-goods. In the Iron Age females are certainly found with arrows and weaponry, at Pokrovka in Russia for example. It is quite possible that a number of women were also buried with Beakers and the warrior package. Beakers failed to make much of an impression in Scandinavia and northern Europe, but in this region a set of exquisite flint daggers was found, dating from *c.* 2200–1800 BC. These daggers were copies of metal equivalents from central Europe and were buried with bodies in stone cists. Stone cists were also prominent in northern Britain and Ireland.

Following the Beaker period, the Early Bronze Age (after *c.* 2000 BC) saw the emergence of 'Tumulus' Cultures involving the burial of individuals, often with rich grave-goods, beneath round barrows. One example of this is the Wessex Culture burials of south-west Britain. Daggers, gold decorative pieces and sceptres were found in such tumuli, as at Bush Barrow near Stonehenge in Wiltshire. Barrows sometimes occurred in quite large cemetery groupings in Britain, the Low Countries (for example the Toterfout Halve Mijl group in the Netherlands) and parts of Denmark and Sweden. They are often sited in prominent positions, and it has been argued that they may have served as territorial markers; they certainly placed the ancestors firmly upon the landscape, perhaps in an attempt to influence later generations.

A series of Early Bronze Age burials in log coffins have been discovered under barrows in Denmark, preserved by the anaerobic conditions of the ground in which they were found. These burials provide the best information so far on the costume of Bronze Age men and women in Europe as in a number of cases clothing has survived in these coffins. (Other elements, such as hair, are also sometimes preserved.) Woven garments including a type of 'kilt', long skirts, cloaks and caps have been recovered from the various graves, alongside grave accoutrements such as horn combs, jewellery and bronzes. A male burial from Muldbjerg wore a long woven woollen cloak, a cap made of several layers of cloth sewn together (sometimes interpreted as a helmet) and a cloth gown, and was equipped with a bronze sword in a wooden sheath. Similar garments were recovered from a grave at Trindhøj. Perhaps the best known of the female coffin burials is that of the Egtved girl. Clad in a woollen top with a string skirt and wrapped in a woollen blanket, this female had a spiked bronze belt-disc and other accessories (Glob 1974).

One of the major changes between the earlier and later periods of the Bronze Age in northern and western European societies was the transition in burial rites from the inhumation traditions discussed above to the predominance of cremations after around 1300 BC. This was the so-called Urnfield Culture, whereby cremated remains were put into ceramic urns and placed in cemeteries or 'Urnfields'. These cemeteries were found across much of Europe, such as Saint-Gond and Aulnay-aux-Planches in France and the Deverel-Rimbury cemetery groups in Britain. Urnfields of regionally differing character were also found in the Late Bronze Age of the Low Countries, for example at Neerpelt-De Roosen. This phenomenon represents a radical shift in attitudes – the body was almost totally reduced by cremation and the grave-goods found in the earlier Tumulus Culture graves were generally absent from the cemeteries of the Urnfield period. This means that the archaeological record more or less dries up with the introduction of the Urnfield Culture.

An interesting variation in cremation rites is found in Scandinavia, mainly on the island of Gotland but with some in Denmark and Norway. Here, ship-setting burials were formed by placing a series of stone slabs in alignment to form the shape of a ship (**Fig. 2.4**), and cremations were often placed within these 'ships'. These astonishing monuments reflect the importance of boats for trade and perhaps indicate raiding taking place in the region. Certainly the use of boats is borne out by the rock carvings of the Scandinavian Bronze Age.

Although bronzes are found in smaller numbers in Late Bronze Age funerary contexts, they occur more abundantly in rivers and lakes. In addition human bones are also found

Fig. 2.4. A ship-setting burial from Boge parish, Gotland, Sweden. (Photo: Antikvarisk-topografiska arkivet, Stockholm)

in rivers, for example the collection of skulls recovered from the River Thames in Britain. This suggests that water-based cults were important in the ritual activities of Late Bronze Age societies and may also explain why we find so few inhumations at this time.

Funerary trends in the region also included burials within large pits and in caves, but the general trend was from inhumation of individuals with grave-goods beneath barrows in the earlier period to cremation without grave-goods in the later Bronze Age. It is difficult to learn much about Bronze Age societies simply from their burial rites, but such burials do reveal some interesting facts relevant to our study – the types of weapons available, for example. Certainly in the Beaker Period it seems to have been important to portray individuals as warriors, while daggers and rapiers are found in the graves of the Tumulus

Culture. By the Late Bronze Age, though, we have far less information as bodies were cremated without goods. Nevertheless the ship-setting burials at least indicate the importance of the boat to northern societies.

Palaeopathology

Without doubt the most poignant evidence for conflict in Bronze Age Europe comes from the remains of its victims. Although skeletons exhibiting weapons injuries are not necessarily proof of warfare (other explanations include executions, murders, immediate post-mortem wounds and even ritual killings), it seems probable that combat is the main explanation. As we have seen, the burial practices of the Bronze Age clearly affect our dataset, with burials under barrows or in log coffins providing us with skeletal material evidence of a type largely absent from most cremations and the rites of the Late Bronze Age. Given the overall paucity of skeletons for study, the subset of human remains showing weapons damage must, by definition, be smaller still. Indeed, death in combat need leave no actual trace on the skeletal remains. Perhaps we are actually excavating the 'illustrious dead', but have no means of ascertaining this. None the less some victims of violent acts are clearly present in the archaeological record and many of the major examples come from the British Isles.

At Barrow Hills in Radley, Oxfordshire, a central grave (Feature 203) held the crouched inhumation of an adult male (**Fig. 2.5**). With this body was a Beaker and a number of barbed and tanged flint arrowheads. Of greatest interest was the presence of one of these arrowheads right next to the spine of the corpse. This arrowhead had an impact fracture at its tip and both of its barbs were broken. There is a distinct possibility that it had caused the death of the individual (Bradley, Chambers & Halpin 1984).

Another victim of archery, an adult male, 25–35 years old, has been recovered from Stonehenge in Wiltshire (**Fig. 2.6**). He lay in a pit which was cut through a ditch and

Fig. 2.5. The skeleton of a male in a Beaker burial at Barrow Hills, Radley, was found to have a flint arrowhead contained within his ribcage; possibly it caused the individual's death. (Photo: Oxford Archaeology Unit)

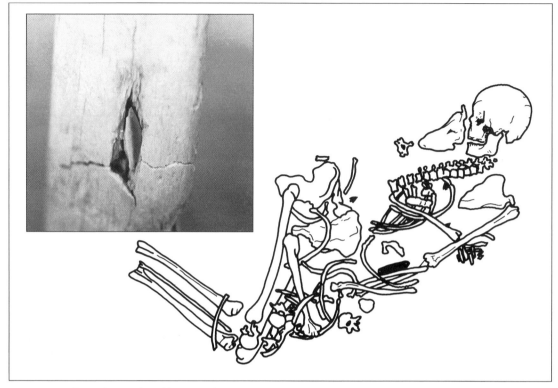

Fig. 2.6. The Beaker Age burial from Stonehenge in Wiltshire, England. The skeleton is accompanied by arrowheads and a bracer. Inset: the flint arrowhead embedded in the fourth left rib of this body. (Photo: Prof. John Evans)

was accompanied by an archer's wristguard. A small flint fragment was embedded in his mesosternum while a rib on his left-hand side contained the tip of a further flint arrowhead. Another arrowhead was found in the back of the sternum, and the excavators believed that this had proved fatal. The arrow had entered the body from the back, hitting the eleventh rib and then passing up through the victim's heart to the sternum. The angles of the projectile points and the force of entry also seemed to indicate that this was close-range combat (Richards 1991: 65; Evans 1984). At Amesbury, again in Wiltshire, a couple of maimed individuals were found under a barrow.

For the later Bronze Age, of course, archaeologists are unable to use skeletons as cremation destroys any evidence of combat. This being said, there is an intriguing cremation from a burial mound at Hogeloon in the Netherlands where a flint arrowhead was found with the cremated remains in a grave probably dating to the Bronze Age. The arrowhead had been badly damaged by the firing process, particularly at its base. It is just possible that this projectile had been the cause of the individual's death and that because the tip of the arrowhead had been embedded within a bone, it had been protected from, and thus less damaged by, the fire (Janssens 1970: 36 and Fig. 9).

Fig. 2.7. A Bronze Age spear embedded in the vertebrae of a young male from Tormarton, South Gloucestershire. (Photo: by courtesy of Bristol City Museums and Art Galleries)

For the latest period of the Bronze Age evidence is even sparser, with no barrows and no cremation cemeteries. Certainly in Britain human remains are very scarce. Despite this, we still do find clear indications of warfare from human remains. At Over Vindinge, Svaerdborg, in Denmark, for example, the remains of a 50–60-year-old man were recovered from a burial. A bronze spearhead around 47mm in length and 24mm wide was found embedded in his pubis, having entered his body from behind (Bennike 1985: 109–10). Although the injury was not the cause of death since new bone had apparently grown around the spearhead, it is a further indication of the use of weapons in the Bronze Age. As the skeleton has now been lost it is impossible to undertake any further analysis, but it seems likely that he suffered this wound in a battle or skirmish which he survived.

An act of extraordinary violence took place at West Littleton Down, Tormarton, in Gloucestershire (Knight, Brown & Grinsell 1972). In 1968 the laying of a gas pipeline disturbed the remains of at least three individuals, two of which had weapons injuries. Skeleton I had a hole in the pelvis made by a lozenge-sectioned spearhead which had been driven into the victim's side as he fell (or perhaps after he had fallen). Skeleton II still had a bronze spearhead embedded in the vertebrae; this would have destroyed the spinal cord, causing immediate paralysis (**Fig. 2.7**). In addition, the tip of another spearhead was discovered in the pelvis of Skeleton II, and the skull was also damaged. Perhaps this man

Fig. 2.8. The Bronze Age linear ditch at Tormarton, South Gloucestershire. The human remains were located in this ditch around 1m from the surface.

had received a blow to the head before being dispatched by spear-thrusts to the body. A Late Bronze Age radiocarbon date was obtained from this skeleton. Further excavation of the site by Richard Osgood in 1999 found further human remains, of at least two individuals, and established that the bodies had all been thrown into a V-shaped ditch around 1.4m in depth (**Fig. 2.8**). The ditch was then backfilled in a single phase with a series of limestone slabs. This ditch was a segment of one of the linear ditches present in the later Bronze Age landscape, with the burials placed close to the terminal.

Another skeleton, discovered in 1901 at Queenford Farm, Dorchester-on-Thames, Oxfordshire, also revealed spear wounds. The pelvis had been pierced by a triangular-bladed basal-looped bronze spearhead, which had broken off when the spear was withdrawn from the corpse. Here again the spear must have been used more in the style of a lance than as a throwing weapon. A radiocarbon date of around 1260–990 BC was obtained from this unfortunate individual (Osgood 1998: 21). An almost identical find has apparently been noted in the museum at Aveyron in southern France. A human skeleton from La Grotte du Pas de Joulie, Trèves (Gard), was found to have the point of a Bronze Age spearhead transfixing its vertebrae (Knight, Brown & Grinsell 1972: 17).

Thus, it seems we have found patterns of possible combat trauma changing through time. In the earlier Bronze Age flint arrowheads and archery dominate, while thrusting spears were the killing weapon of the later period. Again, we should not assume that all wounds are from combat. There are, for example, a number of Iron Age burials in Yorkshire that, on first inspection, suggest death in warfare. One grave at Garton Slack (GS10) contained fourteen spearheads, six of which had been driven into the corpse, the others being scattered around as if hurled into the grave. GS7 had eleven in similar positions, five of which were embedded in the body. In both cases, it seems that the spearheads were thrust into the bodies immediately prior to or after death – a ritual 'killing' of the individual as opposed to their death in combat (Stead 1991). Despite this, however, it is likely that the Bronze Age examples mentioned above were killed in combat.

The burial practices of the Bronze Age and the physical remains they contain are both valuable resources in our argument for the presence of combat. Our examples have been slain by arrows for the most part in the Early Bronze Age and by spears in the Late Bronze Age, though the cases found so far may not reflect the true situation. Warrior status certainly seems to have been important to Bronze Age peoples with groups of weaponry being placed with the dead.

WEAPONRY AND ARMOUR

Bronze weapons represent the defining artefact types of the period, which has been described as the 'first arms race'. At the start of the Bronze Age the major weapons are the bow and arrow and the dagger. As time progresses we see the possible use of the halberd and the emergence of the spear, the rapier and the sword, and by the Urnfield period warriors are protected by armour such as helmets, shields, greaves and breastplates.

Arrowheads were as efficient a killing tool in the Bronze Age as they were in the Middle Ages. Yet the bow was not an innovation of the Bronze Age: it had existed in the Mesolithic and extensive use is known in the Neolithic. But in the Beaker Period it became the definitive symbol of power. Burials are accompanied by archers' wristguards and arrowheads, while Scandinavian rock carvings depict the use of the bow.

Daggers have also been found in numerous graves throughout the region and may have been a functional weapon, though this implies very close combat. Daggers were likely to be a 'one-chance' weapon and the display properties of the item were probably of equal importance to its killing attributes. Perhaps the same can be said for the so-called 'battle-axes' of the Early Bronze Age which may have added to an individual's prestige without necessarily offering a combat advantage. The discovery of flint and even baked clay copies of daggers and axes in Scandinavia reveal the importance of the objects even when bronze was not available.

Through the Bronze Age the dagger changed in form and by the Middle Bronze Age the rapier had been developed. Basically an extended dagger, the rapier was a long, thin thrusting weapon which would have required a degree of training in its use as it required greater precision than daggers or later slashing swords. That rapiers were used in an unsuitable slashing motion, which is a more natural movement, is indicated by the tears found on the rivet holes on the handles of many such weapons.

From dagger to rapier and, ultimately, to sword. Swords appeared in Europe in the later Middle Bronze Age and were commonplace by the Late Bronze Age (**Fig. 2.9**). These

Fig. 2.9. The hilt of an octagonal-hilted sword from Denmark, c. 1500 BC, showing the fine craftsmanship often present on these weapons. This sword may well have been made in the north Alpine region. (Photo: Ashmolean Museum, Oxford)

objects were evidently imbued with mystique and gave great prestige to their owners. Large numbers of the Late Bronze Age swords which have been examined have revealed edge damage, consistent with use in combat (Bridgford 1997). Swords which had been sharpened were certainly useful in combat while those apparently unsharpened examples from the archaeological record could still be seen as vital, extraordinary symbols of power and beauty, perhaps hinting at the martial character of their owner. Sword blades were generally leaf-shaped but hilt forms varied quite significantly. Some were solid while others made use of handle plates of bone or wood. By the end of the Late Bronze Age in the Atlantic Zone of Europe, the 'Carp's Tongue' sword becomes widespread. So-called because of its shape, this tapering weapon combined the stabbing attributes of the rapier with the slashing technology of the leaf-shaped sword to produce a versatile close-combat weapon.

In contrast, the spear was used at slightly longer range by virtue of its wooden shaft. Spears came into use at the end of the Early Bronze Age and can be divided into larger (lance) and smaller (javelin) groups. The smaller spearheads would have been just as deadly in thrusting mode – a fact to which the unfortunates from Tormarton and Dorchester bear testament. Some spears were probably not intended for combat at all, being too large and unwieldy – one from Wandle Park in Croydon was over 80cm long. Others seem to have utilised the principles of encumbrance well before the Roman *pilum* perfected the design. At North Ferriby in Yorkshire archaeologists recovered a large broad-bladed spearhead with pegs on the socket. It is possible that this was used like a harpoon, with the spearhead breaking off in an opponent's shield, leaving the shaft hanging by leather threads and necessitating the discarding of the shield (Bartlett & Hawkes 1965). Clearly spears could be also used in hunting.

The old archaeological saying 'absence of evidence is not evidence of absence' should not be forgotten in our examination of the weapons of the Bronze Age. In addition to the bronze weapons that we do find, there may well have been equally deadly weapons made from organic materials which have not survived in the archaeological record. Certainly there are numerous examples documenting the lethal qualities of wooden clubs. The Maori used *Patu Potu* clubs, made from wood or whalebone, and war clubs were also used by groups such as the Fulani in Nigeria and, famously, the Zulu with their *iwisa* (knobkerries).

Fighting equipment increases and changes throughout the Bronze Age, with bows and arrows and daggers dominating at the start, shifting to rapiers and spears and finally swords and spears. In recent centuries we have seen how developments in offensive technology are countered by advances in defensive capabilities and this situation was no different in the Bronze Age. By the end of the period there was an extensive range of defensive equipment, including shields, helmets, corselets and even greaves, all of which would have provided some protection for the warrior in combat.

Shields

At Kilmahamogue in County Antrim, Ireland, a wooden shield-former that would have been used as a mould for a V-notched leather shield has yielded a radiocarbon date of 1950–1540 BC, a date which indicates that shields were certainly present in western Europe in the Early Bronze Age. In a famous, if rather dangerous, experiment, the archaeologist John Coles illustrated that shields made from organic materials such as leather and wood were actually more functional than their metal equivalents. Hit with a sword in the experiment, the metal shield was almost sliced in half. Thus metal shields may have been intended as 'parade armour', better suited to display than to combat.

Our knowledge of organic defensive equipment is heavily influenced by the survival conditions. Nevertheless wooden U-notch shields have been found at Annandale and Cloonlara in Ireland and have been dated to the eighth century BC. Both had been carved from single slices cut from a tree trunk. A leather shield of the type used by Coles for his demonstration was recovered from Clonbrin, again in Ireland (**Fig. 2.10**). It was some 50cm in diameter and 5–6mm thick, and the handle was stitched on to the back of the

Fig. 2.10. The leather shield from Clonbrin, Ireland. Although some metal shields may have been used in combat, it is probable that wooden and leather variants, such as this example, were far more common. (Photo: National Museum of Ireland, Dublin)

shield with the warrior's hand fitting into the niche left under the raised shield boss (Coles 1962).

Bronze shields are also prominent in the defensive package. Initially they were probably solid cast, and although many would have been too flimsy for use some have clearly seen combat. A Nipperwiese class shield from Long Wittenham in Oxfordshire bears clear battle scars (**Fig. 2.11**). Roughly 396mm average diameter and 1–1.25mm in thickness, this shield had a series of perforations made by spearheads, two of which had been mended by being hammered flat (Needham 1979). Such damage may be linked to a ritual practice – a Yetholm-type Late Bronze Age shield recently found at South Cadbury hillfort in Somerset had been speared while on the ground, while two *phalerae* (horse decorations) from Melksham in Wiltshire display frenzied ritual perforation damage, but nevertheless the use of metal shields for combat should not be dismissed.

A large number of Bronze Age shields have been found in Scandinavia and are often depicted in the region's rock art. Finds have been made at Taarup Mose, Svendstrup, Lommelev Mose, Sørup and other locations in Denmark, and at Nackhälle and the remarkable Fröslunda in Sweden. Here sixteen Herzsprung-type shields were recovered from land that had once been a bog at the edge of a lake. They had been deliberately

Fig. 2.11. The Long Wittenham shield from England. This example of a Nipperwiese-class shield shows clear lozenge-shaped perforations made by a weapon and perhaps inflicted in battle. (Photo: Ashmolean Museum, Oxford)

deposited, perhaps as an offering to deities (Bradley 1998: 7). The very fact that shields are disposed of in a votive fashion in the Bronze Age illustrates their importance and reflects the essential role of the warrior in the period.

Shields were designed for use in arm's-length combat, allowing enough space for a sword blow or spear strike to be made. Once one was close enough to an opponent to use a dagger, a shield was of little protective use. The presence of shields thus fits in with the perceived progression of combat styles from the use of daggers to the use of rapiers and swords.

Helmets, corselets and greaves

In addition to shields, Bronze Age warriors could also call on helmets, corselets and greaves for protection. A series of Late Bronze Age helmets have been recovered from France,

Fig. 2.12. The Viksø horned helmets, found in a peat bog in Denmark. (Photo: National Museum of Denmark, Copenhagen)

primarily from watery locations such as rivers. Helmets with flamboyant crests have been discovered at Auxonne, Blainville-la-Grande, Montmacq and Paris, while a hoard of nine crested helmets was found at Bernières d'Ailly. Such gleaming bronzes were doubtless a potent symbol of a warrior aristocracy, especially when used in conjunction with other defensive accoutrements. The enigmatic Late Bronze Age helmets from a peat bog at Viksø in Denmark (and dated to Montelius Period V at the end of the Bronze Age) clearly testify to the showy nature of bronze display armour (**Fig. 2.12**). These two helmets, probably imported from eastern Europe, both have a pair of curving horns (aesthetically similar to the bronze *lurs* or trumpets of the region) and each also has a face beaten on to it. Two eyes gaze from the front of the helmets, with a hooked beak between them. These fabulous pieces would have been too top-heavy to have had any practical use (*see* Hencken 1971).

France yields the best evidence for body protection, despite the paucity of shield finds. The famous Marmesse cuirass (corselet), magnificently worked with repoussé decoration, dates to the Late Bronze Age (**Fig. 2.13**). Greaves were used to protect the legs, and a fragment of such an object was found in the hoard from Cannes-Écluse (Seine et Marne) of the early Urnfield Period. Taken as a whole, one can picture the Late Bronze Age

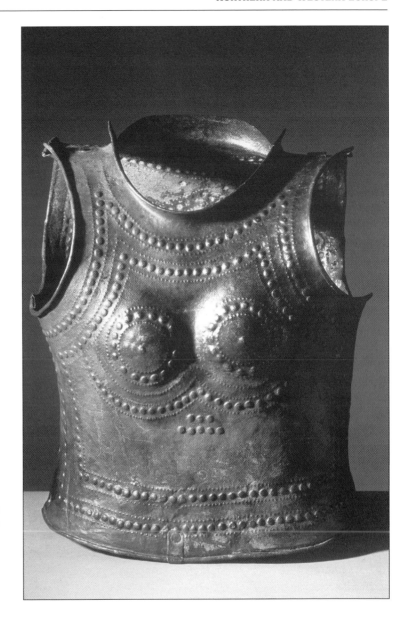

Fig. 2.13. The Marmesse cuirass, France. This beautiful bronze breastplate is made of thin bronze sheet and thus was almost certainly for ceremonial display rather than for actual use in combat. (Photo: RMN – Jean Schormans)

(Urnfield) warrior bedecked with helmet, greaves and shield, and armed with sword and/or spear. Bronze protective items were probably used mainly for display, and it is likely that more functional examples made from leather co-existed with them. This being said, Anthony Harding has pointed out that the mere sight of Patroclus wearing Achilles' bronze armour struck fear into the hearts of the Trojans (*Iliad*, Book XVI) – a possible raison d'être for Bronze Age 'parade' armour.

As the Bronze Age progressed weapons became technologically more advanced, and these advances not only necessitated changes in defensive technologies, but also facilitated them. By the onset of the succeeding Iron Age, the Bronze Age warrior was able to call upon a wide range of defensive protection while making use of a varied arsenal of beautiful yet deadly bronze weapons.

ICONOGRAPHY

Bronze Age rock carvings have been studied in detail and can add much to our knowledge of warfare in the period. Especially prominent are the carvings of Scandinavia, tentatively dated to around 1000 BC. Although they depict much more than just images of warriors and fighting, these carvings do illustrate much of the weaponry discussed above. Swords, bows, spears and axes are all portrayed, together with illustrations of the defensive equipment (**Fig. 2.14**). Round shields appear in abundance and some individuals seem to be wearing horned helmets of the type found at Viksø. John Coles has suggested that the carvings of warriors with 'square' bodies may in fact be portraying bulky padded armour, while those with thickened calves may perhaps be wearing greaves of a type similar to that found at Cannes-Écluse (*see* Coles 1990).

France, too, has pictorial representations of note. A famous example from Substantion (Hérault), which may be a funeral stele, has an excellent depiction of a notched shield. Above this is what may be a spear and a series of (?chariot) wheels (**Fig. 2.14(a)**). This carving is in a similar style to many from southern Spain (*see* Chapter Three).

Beyond the actual presence of warriors and weaponry, can the rock carvings really tell us anything about the nature of fighting? Perhaps they reveal preferred combinations of weapons. For example, shields are depicted with all weapon types apart from the bow; this is quite logical, since the bow requires the use of both hands. Some figures are shown with an extensive panoply of sword, shield, axe and helmet. Fighting scenes rarely seem to show more than three individuals and combat between pairs is the norm. It is possible that these carvings depict the display of weaponry and ritual ceremonies rather than actual combat – a celebration of champions and of heroes with their wondrous bronze armour and mystical weapons. Certainly, there are no images that could clearly be interpreted as an armed raid.

Although they are more frequently shown on dry land, it is interesting to note that boats are often depicted (**Fig. 2.14(b)**). Armed individuals on these vessels may provide an intriguing hint as to the nature of conflict – raiding by sea or river along the trade-routes of the period, as was suggested above. Horses are also present in the Scandinavian carvings with vehicles of chariot-type. One image from Tegneby, Northern Bohuslän, shows a number of mounted warriors armed with spears and shields, perhaps engaged in combat (although this may be Iron Age in date). The increased use of the horse towards the end of the Bronze Age might have been significant in providing warriors with far greater mobility and the ability to cover greater distances. Perhaps the presence of mounted warriors provides an explanation for another feature found in certain carvings: chapes. These were curved attachments fixed to the end of scabbards, enabling a mounted warriors to remove his sword from its sheath by placing a foot on the chape while withdrawing the weapon. For a footsoldier, of course, such an object is unnecessary. Chapes are probably shown with warriors in Kville Hundred, Sweden (**Fig. 2.14c and d**). Horses may have increased the mobility of war bands, but combat would have taken place

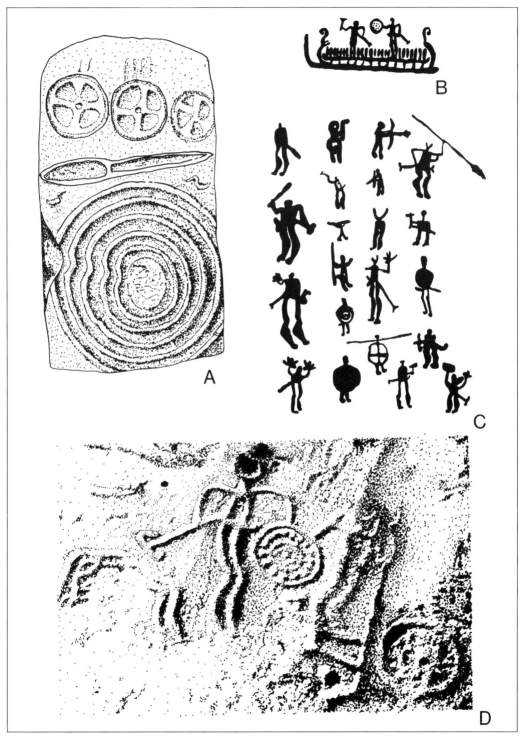

Fig. 2.14. Bronze Age rock-carvings. (a) Substantion, France; (b) and (c) Kville Hundred, Sweden; (d) Heden, Kville, Sweden.

on foot; horses at this time were much smaller than today's typical cavalry horse, being more the size of an Exmoor pony.

Although we cannot assume the direct portrayal of combat types in these carvings, they do seem to provide useful pointers to the types of weaponry in use. Perhaps they also hint at the increasing importance of boats and mounted 'infantry' as raiding became more prevalent in the later Bronze Age.

CONCLUSIONS

The various strands discussed above can be drawn together to provide a cogent picture of the progression in styles of warfare through the Bronze Age in northern and western Europe. The weaponry clearly shows changes through time. Initially, the bow and arrow seemed to dominate, as is borne out by the so-called archer's package with the Beaker burials. Daggers were the primary bladed weapon of the early Bronze Age and these developed first into rapiers and ultimately into swords. The sword was certainly the prestige weapon of the Late Bronze Age, an object of great aesthetic importance as well as a deadly tool in the right hands. The leaf-shaped swords of the Urnfield Period show a clear break in technologies from the thrusting rapiers of the Tumulus Culture. In the *Iliad*, Homer depicts the meeting of bronze-clad champions (or heroes) doing battle to the death. This type of combat would certainly be more suited to the Tumulus Culture – the rapier is the weapon of a champion, requiring precision and training in its use. As the sword develops, so does the more natural weapon in a slashing action, probably practised by a warrior elite. Ultimately the Carp's Tongue sword provided an all-round weapon with both stabbing and slashing attributes.

In the Middle Bronze Age spears replace arrowheads as the dominant projectile weapon. The smaller spearheads were more suitable for projectile/javelin purposes, while the larger spearheads were better suited to thrusting/lance use. The dead of Tormarton and Dorchester, as we have said, tell a very different story. Smaller spearheads could be used just as effectively for stabbing purposes and thus were a very versatile weapon in close and longer-range combat.

The panoply of defensive arms changed dramatically too. An Early to Middle Bronze Age date for the shield-former from Kilmahamogue indicates early origins. It seems that shields, whether of leather, wood or metal, were an important part of the warrior's equipment in the Tumulus Culture period. It also seems that such shields were more prevalent in Britain and Scandinavia while helmets were more common in France. As metalworking techniques improved, so did the potential for elaborate, showy protection. Helmets were, of course, just one element, along with greaves and corselets. The full assemblage of protective bronzes and weaponry may never have been used in anger, and certainly some elements were too weak to survive any blows. Instead more practical defensive alternatives, fashioned in leather or wood, were used for actual combat while the bronzes were kept for display in votive rituals to reflect prestige upon the owner. Parade armour was the domain of a warrior elite (**Fig. 2.15**).

With the change from Tumulus Culture to Urnfield Culture we see not only a change in the assemblage of weaponry and protective gear but also an increase in the construction of

Fig. 2.15. The Late Bronze Age warrior. (Simon Pressey)

defences. Lowland settlements were provided with stronger barriers while the hilltops were sometimes given quite substantial fortifications. The general dividing up of the landscape from the later Middle Bronze Age onwards and the provision of defences reflect competition over land – an increasingly scarce resource. In addition, prestige goods were frequently made in these hilltop settlements, which perhaps served as places of exchange as well as providing protection for agricultural communities. Often constructed in dominant positions overlooking riverine trade-routes, these sides were the forerunners of the larger Iron Age hillforts and the *oppida*. Some archaeologists have suggested that hillforts were not constructed for practical defensive purposes, rather that they were religious centres where ritual practices took place and the landscape was controlled. Material found in the ditches of some of these sites, such as moulds for prestige objects, seems to indicate that defence was not their only purpose, and certainly there may well be some truth in this for certain sites since 'statements in soil' on such a scale could reflect prestige on those constructing them. Having said that, the construction of a simple bank and ditch would provide a degree of practical defence and, given the apparent increase in weaponry types, it is certainly possible that protection against attack was a prime motive in the building of many of these sites.

Evidence for an attack on a Bronze Age hillfort in western or northern Europe has not so far been found, but attacks were made on Neolithic and Iron Age sites, and we must not assume that we shall not find such evidence in the future.

What form did conflict take in the Bronze Age of northern and western Europe? It is difficult to be too dogmatic on this point based on information derived solely from the archaeological record. Certainly the weaponry of the earlier period is often more suited to the fighting of champions in true Homeric fashion, using weapons such as daggers and later rapiers. This type of combat may have been quite carefully choreographed and different from other forms of conflict. Bows were used for fighting as well as for hunting, and larger-scale raids may have been common as elites tried to grab prestige goods from the extensive trading networks. In either scenario, a select group probably undertook the actual fighting.

In the later Bronze Age static defences appear, and with them the slashing leaf-shaped swords and more armour. The build-up of wealth, in terms of both trade and agricultural production, in certain areas, combined with the dividing up of the landscape with linear ditches and field systems, led to increased raiding and aggressive competition. Static resources became more valuable, and thus more likely to be attacked by war-bands, and so required the defences that are such a feature in the Late Bronze Age of the region.

Mobility would have been vital to any Late Bronze Age groups intent on raiding defended centres or settlements – the most important means of transport being boats and horses. Goods were moved over large distances along the trade-routes by boat and presumably by carts and wagons. Examples of boats have been found at Dover and North Ferriby in Britain. Boats were hugely important, and their significance is reflected in their frequent portrayal in the rock-carvings of Scandinavia. In addition, a curious wooden object from Roos Carr in Humberside depicts a series of figures on a boat holding circular (and thus possibly Bronze Age) shields (**Fig. 2.16**). A Late Bronze Age/Early Iron Age

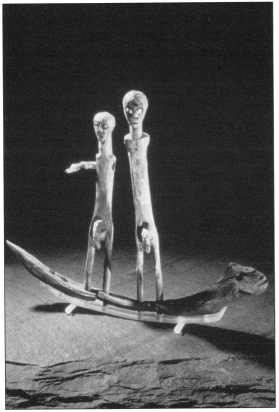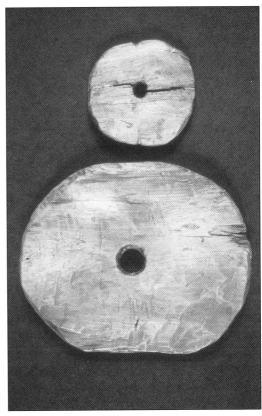

Fig. 2.16. The Roos Carr warriors from Humberside, England. These wooden figures were standing on a small wooden boat, and were probably holding shields (right). They may well be an early depiction of a raiding party. (Photo: Hull City Museums, Art Galleries and Archives)

radiocarbon date has been obtained for this and so the figures may well represent Bronze Age warriors on a boat. If trade goods could pass along a river by boat, then so could warriors attempting to snatch the goods, or perhaps using the river as a 'highway' to attack centres of production or to seize land – hence the increased provision of defences. A number of the defensive sites of the period are situated on rivers, perhaps to counter the effects of such raids. Although Iron Age in date, a fascinating boat was excavated at Hjortspring in Denmark; on board was found the equipment of a sizeable raiding party with many weapons (Randsborg 1995). Perhaps this is a later example of the type of raiding parties used in the Late Bronze Age.

FURTHER READING

Bradley, R. 1998. *The Passage of Arms: an archaeological analysis of prehistoric hoards and votive deposits* (Oxbow)

Carman, J. & Harding, A.F. 1999. *Ancient Warfare* (Sutton)

Coles, J.M. 1962. 'European Bronze Age Shields', *Proceedings of the Prehistoric Society* 28, 156–90

Coles, J.M. & Harding A.F. 1979. *The Bronze Age in Europe* (Methuen)

Hencken, H. 1971. *The Earliest European Helmets: Bronze Age and Early Iron Age* (Peabody Museum, Harvard University)

Knight, R.W., Browne, C. & Grinsell, L.V. 1972. 'Prehistoric skeletons from Tormarton', *Transactions of the Bristol & Gloucester Archaeological Society* 91, 14–17

Mercer, R. 1999. 'The origins of warfare in the British Isles', in J. Carman & A.F. Harding (eds), *Ancient Warfare* (Sutton)

Osgood, R.H. 1998. *Warfare in the Late Bronze Age of North Europe* (British Archaeological Reports Int. Series 694)

THREE

SPAIN

INTRODUCTION

Many general studies of Europe overlook the Iberian peninsula (Spain and Portugal) and the study of warfare is no exception. Some regard Iberia as 'peripheral' (and in some cases, backward) to the rest of continental Europe and events taking place there. Many scholars perceive its archaeology to be difficult both to interpret and to link to wider changes in the rest of Europe. One reason for this is the problem of accessibility: excavation reports and syntheses of evidence are most often published as short papers in Spanish and Portuguese journals, and therefore such information rarely reaches a wide audience. Another problem is Iberia's extreme diversity. Made up of a series of provinces, its geography, topography, vegetation, climate, natural resources and, of course, archaeology vary enormously from north to south and from east to west. This means that it is often difficult to generalise about the peninsula as a whole. More general studies of the archaeological evidence from Iberia are clearly needed and it is hoped that this chapter goes some way to this end.

Although Iberia is 'different' and the fieldwork carried out there has perhaps progressed at a slower rate than much of Europe, this chapter will show that the archaeological record is very rich in its own right. Furthermore, there are many striking similarities between the Bronze Age cultures and archaeological material of Iberia and those of the rest of Europe.

This chapter focuses specifically on evidence for warfare from Spain. Compared with other areas of Europe, very little work on the Bronze Age in Spain has been published in English, and undertaking a study such as this means piecing together evidence from a vast array of articles, excavation and survey reports. It is important to note that, just as the regions of Spain are highly varied, so are the amount and quality of the investigations carried out there. Some areas, particularly the south-east, have been the subject of intensive survey, with many excavation projects, although the same cannot be said of many regions in the north. Also, many of the key sites that we rely on to build historical and cultural sequences were excavated early in the twentieth century when techniques were very different to those of the present day and many finds were discarded, to be lost forever.

Evidence for warfare in Bronze Age Spain comes from a range of different types of data: settlement patterns, fortifications, weapons and armour, skeletal remains and rock art. In the past archaeological investigations into the prehistoric period tended to concentrate on excavating large defended settlements. Although these fortifications were often described in detail, their function and wider significance in terms of warfare were not considered.

There were in fact virtually no studies of prehistoric warfare in Spain until very recently (Monks 1998; Oosterbeek 1997). Many of the best-known fortified sites were discovered in south-east Spain at the end of the nineteenth century and in the early 1900s by two Belgian mining engineers working in the area, Henri and Louis Siret. In the absence of accurate dating methods they, and later others, attributed the apparent 'sudden' appearance of these fortified sites to influences or direct implantation from the more advanced civilisations of the east. Louis Siret thought these people could have been the Phoenicians, while later scholars believed that it was the Mycenaeans who brought these fortifications to the peninsula, along with new methods of burial and items of material culture. With the advent of radiocarbon dating and subsequent discoveries, it became clear that the fortified sites of Spain were earlier than those of the Phoenicians and Mycenaeans and therefore they must have been built by local groups. This said, there was no attempt to investigate *why* these fortified settlements suddenly appeared in the Copper Age, or how they were built and by whom.

Hundreds of radiocarbon dates are now available from across Spain; these help to accurately date not only individual stratigraphical sequences, the history of events and length of occupation at various sites, but also local and regional cultural sequences. Dates for the Bronze Age vary between different regions owing to the uneven adoption of new types of material culture items (as opposed to maintaining existing traditions), and to problems in identifying the objects that represent the beginning and end of the various phases of the period. The situation is further complicated by the fact that dates for the Bronze Age have not been published for all areas of the peninsula (Castro Martínez, Lull & Micó 1996).

Dates for the Copper Age begin in the early fourth millennium BC and the period ends in the mid- to late third millennium with the Beaker Phase. Although the transitional phase is blurred by uneven adoption and by continued use of Beaker elements in some areas after the phase has ended elsewhere, the Bronze Age in Spain largely begins around 2000–1800 BC. Earlier dates do exist from a number of sites, suggesting that Bronze Age features were adopted earlier in some regions than others. Groups in the south-east were among the first to adopt certain features of the Bronze Age, such as individual burials, new metal objects and new types of settlement, from *c.* 2100 BC onwards. The Early Bronze Age spans from *c.* 1800 to 1500 BC, the Middle Bronze Age from *c.* 1500 to 1200 BC and the Late Bronze Age from *c.* 1200 to 900 BC. The final phase of the Bronze Age had largely ended by *c.* 900–600 BC, a period defined by more intense contacts with other parts of the Mediterranean and Europe which continued into the Early Iron Age. This contact resulted in the introduction of new object types, new technologies, changes in burials and settlements, and the establishment of Phoenician colonies on the south coast.

Neolithic and Copper Age

The earliest defended settlements found in Spain come from the Copper Age. They vary enormously in size, layout, raw materials, construction techniques, sophistication of design, defensive tactics and the amount of investment in building and maintaining the defences. The largest and best known site, Los Millares in Almería, boasted three

Fig. 3.1. The fortification ditch surrounding Fort 1, Los Millares, Almería. (Photo: Sarah Monks)

enclosure walls, towers, bastions, an elaborate entrance and, in a later period, a series of twelve outlying forts (**Fig. 3.1**), while others comprised a single enclosure wall or a central watchtower. The walls, towers and bastions of the Copper Age were typically constructed of stone and mudbrick, although there is some evidence for the use of timber superstructures, perhaps elevated walkways or parapets. These fortified sites used naturally defended positions where possible. Many were located on hilltops or scarps with the advantages of better visibility and increased impregnability – positions that would be hard to attack but easy to defend. Evidence from settlement patterns and studies of the relationship between fortified and non-fortified sites suggests that many Copper Age sites were evenly spaced along watercourses and occupied strategic positions for monitoring other groups and for protecting access to natural resources. In some cases it appears that large well-defended sites, such as Los Millares and El Malagón in the south-east, were surrounded by strategically placed hilltop or 'satellite' sites which added a second line of protection. The amount of investment in some of the larger defended sites was significant and would have required the cooperation of the local community. This, and the location of domestic houses within and between the lines of defence, suggests that they were designed and built for the protection of the whole group. Some defended sites were in use for hundreds of years, with many phases of repair, redesign and elaboration of the defences, but other sites were destroyed or abandoned relatively soon after their initial occupation. Evidence of fire damage, sometimes directly affecting the defences, is also found, suggesting that destruction by fire was a strategy used in inter-group fighting. The individual defensive features – towers, bastions, arrow-slits, complex entrances and blind walls – were all geared towards the use of archery. This is corroborated by the large number of arrowheads found in this period (and the lack of other recognisable weapons), and the skeletal and iconographical evidence.

Cave paintings from before the Bronze Age depict warriors and their weapons. The most common weapon portrayed is the bow and arrow, used in both hunting and inter-group fighting. Some of the scenes depicted show groups of warriors engaged in battle. The first true flint arrowheads are found from the Late Neolithic onwards and a series of technological changes towards greater efficiency can be seen. A greater variety of types (different shapes and styles) and raw materials were used in their production, with some examples being made from non-local 'exotic' stone obtained through inter-group trade. These arrowheads were not only used for fighting and hunting, but have also been found as grave-goods, often in large numbers and with a wide variety of types and materials represented. Evidence for the actual use of these arrowheads in fighting as well as hunting comes from the discovery of flint arrowheads lodged in the bones of human remains from this period (see p. 46).

Our current knowledge of Copper Age society suggests that this was a time of great uncertainty, instability and hostility. Many significant changes were taking place: a greater degree of sedentism as groups settled in more permanent communities and settlements; an increased reliance on agriculture to provide subsistence needs; and population growth. All these factors led to greater competition among closely settled groups and increased hostility and inter-group fighting. The adoption of, and long-term investment in, settlement defences, the choice of locations with good natural defences and visibility, the development of more efficient weapons, the representations of fighting, warriors and their weapons in cave paintings, and skeletal evidence of injuries and violent deaths all suggest an increasingly warlike society.

The Beaker Phase and Transition to the Bronze Age

The final stages of the Copper Age are characterised by the appearance of new objects, changes in the distribution and design of settlements and in the burial record.

Traditionally the Beaker package in Spain consists of a new style of pottery (new vessel forms, shapes and decorative styles), archer's wristguards, V-perforated buttons and a range of new metal objects. This group of objects is considered to form a new set of prestige goods originating in continental Europe, whose possession denoted high status and was concerned with feasting, competition and displays of power and authority.

The end of the Copper Age also saw changes in many other areas of life. Many sites were abandoned and newly founded settlements were generally more dispersed and had greater natural defences, moving away from the linear and often clustered patterns of the Copper Age. The continued use of artificial defences suggests that warfare was still present within society, although different schemes and tactics were adopted. Investment in burial monuments was also reduced in this period as we see a general shift from collective burial in above-ground monuments, to individual or double burials in a less conspicuous form. Labour, materials and time were now invested into the production of wealth items which were being conspicuously deposited in graves and hoards, and were also traded and exchanged between groups.

In the past Spanish scholars have argued that the transition from the Copper Age to the Bronze Age did not take place in a climate of peace and that warfare 'proper' does not become evident within societies until this time. This argument is largely based on the construction of forts in the last phase of occupation at the Copper Age site of Los Millares, the presence of warrior burials early in the Bronze Age and especially in the south-east, and the array of weapons being produced. 'The concentration of acropoles, together with the weaponry in the graves, suggests that militarism was more important in the social landscape of Argaric times than in that of earlier periods' (Gilman & Thornes 1985: 22–3). Recent research (Monks 1997; 1998) has shown that warfare, warriors and weapons were very much part of a pre-Bronze Age society and it is only a lack of investigation that has led to this misunderstanding. However, there are significant changes in the nature and perhaps the frequency of warfare in the Bronze Age, trends that are both interesting and compelling – and require explanation. The emergence of 'warrior graves' in the Early Bronze Age reflects a new era of symbolism and status for the warrior, although it does not necessarily imply that fighting had escalated. Evidence relating to the warfare practised in the Bronze Age is discussed below, and we begin by looking at perhaps the most obvious piece of evidence for the presence of warfare – artificial defences. A number of questions can be raised: Do we see an increase in the degree to which sites were fortified, or do existing traditions continue relatively unchanged? What sort of defensive features were used and how do these relate to changes in fighting tactics and developments in weaponry?

SETTLEMENT PATTERNS AND FORTIFICATIONS

In the Early Bronze Age a number of regional cultures developed which are characterised and differentiated by their material culture and different types of site. For example, that of the south-east is known as the Argaric, named after the type site of El Argar, discovered by the Siret brothers; the region of La Mancha is known as the 'Cultura de las Motillas' after a series of characteristic fortified sites called *motillas* (discussed below). New types of site and changes in the preferred locations for settlement herald the beginning of the Bronze Age in many regions of Spain. In the south-east especially, many sites were abandoned early in the Bronze Age, although in other areas this pattern was less immediate and existing traditions continued for some time. The new settlement patterns that emerged were generally more dispersed, with smaller sites occupying more strategic locations in terms of access to and control over resources and natural routes of communication, and better naturally defended positions. This was coupled with an increase in the economic specialisation of sites, so that some sites were geared towards metallurgical activities, for example, others towards agriculture or animal husbandry. Although settlements were generally further apart and exploited a wider variety of ecological zones, thus reducing local competition, naturally defensive locations were still preferred for the foundation of new settlements and artificial defences continued to be built. A large number of walled settlements existed in the second millennium BC across Spain, though with varying degrees of permanence; some were in use over a significant period of time, while others were occupied only for a hundred years or so.

In general the defensive systems employed, the types of location chosen and the configuration of structures are all different from those of the Copper Age. For the first time, defensive considerations took priority over ease of access to natural resources such as water and cultivable land. In the Bronze Age the majority of sites had some form of defence, whether natural or artificial. At many sites the defensive structures reflect a more sophisticated degree of planning and building skills, for example in many instances they were designed and built in conjunction with the natural topography. The site of Cerro del Salto de Miralrio in the region of Jaén was built on two high platforms surrounded by stone walls, except where a steep drop or the presence of natural rock outcrops made additional defences unnecessary. Later building phases relating to the raising and widening of these walls incorporated new design solutions to problems encountered in adding corridors and entrances to a steep location. The reason for such major defences at this site can perhaps be gleaned from its location; like many Bronze Age sites in the south-east, Cerro del Salto de Miralrio was located at the junction of four diverse and important ecological niches: river, pasture, fertile plain and mineral sources. It was part of a local network of sites geared towards the exploitation of nearby mineral resources, creating strong competition over access to local sources.

There existed enormous differences between sites in the south-east and those in the rest of the peninsula throughout much of the Bronze Age. The Early Bronze Age Argaric sites of the south-east have been described as 'proto-urban', with a nucleated population living in rectilinear complexes arranged on terraces, amid heavily protected citadels and strongly defended locations (**Figs 3.2, 3.3**). On the whole, settlement defences (where they existed) were no longer designed to protect an entire settlement or the majority of the population as they had been in the Copper Age, but instead enclosed a form of citadel or 'acropolis', usually situated at the highest point. The most common artificial defences were stone walls built to complement the natural defensive features of the location or to enclose a citadel area. These walls were often reinforced with towers, the semi-circular bastions of the Copper Age largely being replaced by circular towers in the Bronze Age. Domestic houses were no longer discrete and separate buildings set in their own space, but were arranged in

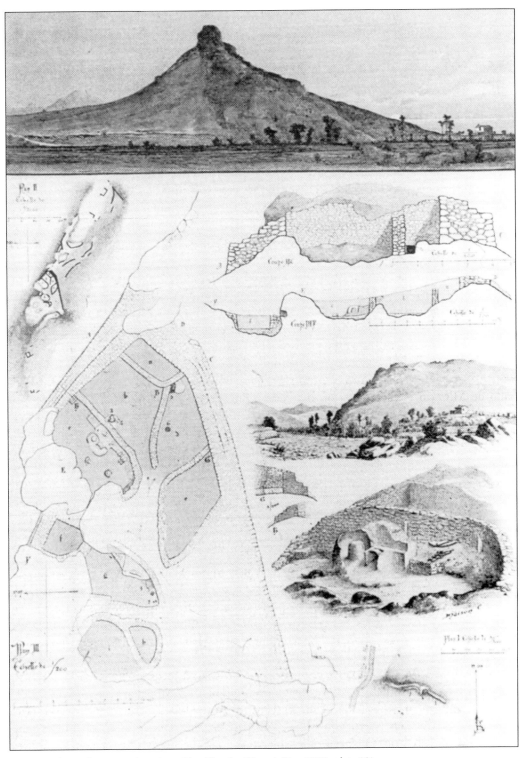

Fig. 3.2. The Early Bronze Age site at Ifre, Murcia. (Siret & Siret 1887: plate 18)

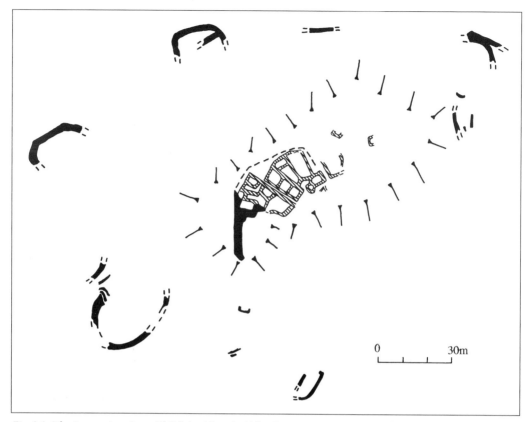

Fig. 3.3. The Bronze Age site at El Oficio, Almería. (After Leira Jimenez 1987: 206, fig. 2)

compartmentalised 'urban' units with rectilinear walls, inter-connecting corridors and steps – 'labyrinthine'-type defences. This also formed a useful line of defence or at least a significant obstacle to an invading force. At the site of Fuente Alamo in Almería most of the domestic housing was located on terraces situated on the sides of the hill. The uppermost area was delimited by fortification walls for the protection of the citadel, which was reserved for a small section of the population and a small number of burials. These changes reflect the existence of a more highly organised and managed social system and the reorganisation of labour expenditure and investment, as exemplified by the Argaric sites. The site of Peñalosa in the region of Jaén was situated on a long spur overlooking the meeting-point of two rivers; the steep drops on either side were artificially terraced. The complex series of buildings on these terraces was enclosed by a large stone wall with bastions which are remarkably well preserved in the eastern sector of the site.

The Bronze Age in the region known as La Mancha (south-central Spain) – an area strongly influenced by the Argaric culture of the south-east – is characterised by permanent, heavily fortified sites known as *motillas*. Typically situated on a conical hill on a low-lying plain, dominating the surrounding area, *motillas* are always located near river courses and/or cultivable land. Many also lie on escarpments, promontories and steep hills, but others had little natural defence which meant that some form of artificial fortification was required. Their dimensions range between 4 and 11 metres high and 40 and 100 metres in diameter, with a square or rectangular central tower up to 6 metres in height. The Motilla del Azuer is the best preserved and most widely studied example. It consists of an exterior wall, up to 5.8 metres wide in places, with at least four phases of construction/ reconstruction in places. A large ditch fills the area between this exterior wall and an inner wall. A number of graves, typical of the Early to Middle Bronze Age, were built into the fortification walls of the site. Open spaces between the fortifications were used for a variety of purposes including habitation, production and processing of foodstuffs, craft activities and storage.

In many other areas of Spain the settlement evidence is not well defined for the Bronze Age. In the north and north-east a variety of settlement types existed, from small dispersed settlements to larger nucleated sites, and from naturally defended hilltop locations to sites enclosed by stone walls. The lack of archaeological survey and excavation in many of these areas has meant that it is difficult to generalise about settlement patterns as a whole. Our knowledge of Bronze Age groups in the south-west, for example, largely comes from graves, stelae, hoards and chance finds, and only recently have excavations of settlements been undertaken. We therefore have to rely on evidence from a small number of well-investigated sites. Essentially the settlement types in this area of Spain are diverse according to their different economic functions, therefore fortified central sites existed alongside farming villages and hillforts. There seems to be some correlation between sites where metalworking took place and the presence of artificial defences. The site of Setefilla in Sevilla, for example, was situated close to mineral resources, good pasture in the mountains and land of good agricultural potential in the lowland valleys. The site is practically inaccessible from the plain and visually dominates a wide area of the nearby river valley, controlling the confluences and natural land routes to the mountains, and the presence and scale of its fortifications make it stand out from other local sites. First occupied in the Middle Bronze Age, the site rapidly developed with the construction of rectangular stone and mudbrick structures and fortification walls with bastions. The earliest occupation phase was destroyed by fire in *c.* 1570 BC, but this was followed by rapid rebuilding. The site was occupied through to the Final Bronze Age, which corresponds to a period of major architectural, economic, social and demographic development, technological improvements in craft production and the adoption of styles and objects of Phoenician origin.

There is little change in settlement patterns and site types until the end of the Bronze Age. After about 1600 BC many fortifications were destroyed and large numbers of sites were abandoned. Newly founded sites were generally more dispersed, less structured and well ordered, and were less preoccupied with defence. Very few new fortifications were built, and there emerges a clear dichotomy between the strategically located defended sites, usually controlling access to metal sources, and more dispersed rural settlements.

BURIAL AND SKELETAL EVIDENCE

Perhaps the most irrefutable evidence for warfare should come from burials, more especially from the study of skeletal remains, but only a few examples of injuries and deaths from the Spanish Bronze Age can be conclusively attributed to violence. Often the indicators are inconclusive and the injuries could have been the result of an accident as much as violence (*see* Chapter One). The study and scientific analysis of skeletal remains in Spain has been carried out as a matter of course only in the past few years and many projects have been slow to publish their results. Where skeletons were encountered in early excavations the remains were often discarded without being properly studied and recorded, and many burials had already been disturbed and/or looted. Osteological studies are now widely carried out on remains from modern excavations in Spain, and their context recorded in detail, although little work has yet been done on collating this information.

There are a number of examples of skeletal injuries and incidences of violent death from Neolithic and Copper Age burials. These typically involve flint arrowheads embedded in some part of the skeleton. It is clear that, in some cases, the individual survived the injury and bone regrowth is evident. In others' death was instantaneous or inevitable. Examples where injury or death was caused by arrowheads, or where they remain lodged in the skeleton, come from a number of sites: Cartuja de las Fuentes (Ebro Basin); Venta del Griso (Teruel); Hipogeo de Longar (Viana, Navarra); San Juan Ante Portam Latinam (Laguardia, Álava); San Quirce del Valles (Barcelona); Cueva de las Cáscaras (Cantabria) (Etxeberria & Vegas 1988a; Campillo 1995). At the cave site of Cueva del Baranco de la Higuera (Baños de Fortuna, Murcia) lesions made by a hard angular object were found on the cranium of one individual. Although some bone regeneration had begun, the individual may not have survived the attack. At the Copper Age site of Valencina de la Concepción (Sevilla) two skeletons had been thrown into a ditch without any funerary ritual or special treatment. The remains were largely articulated although one was missing its head, the other a limb. The seemingly violent nature of their death, the careless method of disposal, evidence of burning from surrounding areas and the possibility that the ditch formed part of the defence of the settlement perhaps all imply a violent attack on the site. The presence of unusual burial treatment is also recorded at the Neolithic site of San Quirce del Valles (Barcelona). Here, a circular pit containing two almost complete male skeletons was found, which appeared unusual when compared to contemporary traditions, and the pit seemed to have been filled rapidly following the deposition of bodies. Both skulls had been intentionally crushed, either while the men were still alive or shortly after death, there were no accompanying grave-goods or funerary ritual and the grave pit itself appears to have been 'improvised'. The collective burial at San Juan Ante Portam Latinam (Laguardia, Álava), dating to the fourth millennium BC, contained up to 336 individuals who were probably all deposited at the same time; they included eight examples with identifiable skeletal injuries and/or traumas caused by arrowheads. This may be the earliest example of a massacre from Spain (Etxeberria & Vegas 1988b; Etxeberria, Herrasti & Vegas 1995).

The few definite examples where death or injury was caused by a violent attack were almost all caused by arrowheads. This confirms the picture of warfare gleaned from the evidence of settlement defences, the cave paintings and weapons recovered from sites that the bow and arrow was the main weapon of attack prior to the Bronze Age.

In the Early Bronze Age we see the emergence of social differentiation in the richness of grave-goods deposited with individuals and the shift to individual, double and triple burials in cists, pits and urns. These graves were often built into walls or placed beneath the floors of dwellings, and replaced the collective burials of the Copper Age which were typically placed within specially built funerary monuments. The social status, power and authority of the individual, or his/her association with a powerful group, were displayed through items deposited with the body, such as bronze weapons and high-status ceramic vessels. In the later Bronze Age, at a time when foreign influences were penetrating the Iberian peninsula, we see the deposition of foreign 'exotic' objects and those made of non-local raw materials.

For the Bronze Age, examples of violent injury and/or death are equally sparse and diverse, and their interpretation as the result of violence, let alone warfare, is difficult. Broad studies collating this type of information are still in their infancy. However, taking into account the array of weapons present in the Bronze Age and the symbolic importance of warfare in iconography and burial rites, we should expect to encounter at least some examples. It seems likely that this general absence of evidence can be attributed to three key factors. First, warfare in Bronze Age society had taken on greater symbolic properties, especially among the elite, and this elite class was most probably increasingly less involved in fighting. Second, it is clear that not all members of society received burial in an identifiable or high-profile manner, and therefore the 'ordinary' warriors killed in battle may have gone unnoticed. (Instead we tend to focus on the elite and the symbols of their power, authority and status.) Third, the changes in weaponry in the Early Bronze Age brought changes in the nature of fighting, its style and tactics. Whereas the injuries caused by arrowheads in earlier periods are easily identified, those caused by cutting and thrusting weapons are more difficult to detect. Furthermore, it could be argued that wounds caused by sharp implements would have been easier to treat, and were perhaps less likely to be fatal than a deeply embedded arrowhead.

There are two main types of burial that provide us with information on the nature of warfare. First, there are the rich warrior burials which include a rich array of weapons – grave-goods that appear to have been largely symbolic, representative of power and status, and perhaps of success in war. Second, there are the burials which contain the remains of those actually killed or injured during fighting, often referred to as 'deviant' burials because they differ from the typical burials of the period. Evidence from the deviant burials sometimes shows that they were dug and covered hastily, often lacking grave-goods and the customary funerary ritual administered to other individuals. On rare occasions we find skeletons lying in ditches or near fortification walls; these presumably relate to individuals who died and became buried where they fell.

Stone or metal arrowheads were found lodged in skeletons from a number of sites: flint arrowheads at La Atalayuela (Rioja), and metal arrowheads at Dolmen de Collet Su (Lleida); Cueva H. de Arboli, (Tarragona) and Grajal de Campos (Leon) (Etxeberria & Vegas 1988a; Campillo 1995). At the site of El Puig, Alcoy (Alicante), a forty-year-old male sustained a curved fracture to the back of the head, most likely made by a sharp cutting implement such as a sword or axe. The edges of the wound showed signs of bone regeneration, proving that the individual had survived the injury. Another individual was found dumped in a ditch at Carrelasvegas; his foot was missing and there were no grave-goods present. Among a group of burials found in the Manzanares valley one skeleton that was excavated from a pit (rather than the usual cist-type burials) was positioned differently from the others interred nearby and stones had been thrown or placed on top of the body; there were no grave-goods. A disarticulated body, with possible cut-marks on the bones, was recorded from the same group of burials. An adult male found at the site of Cerro de la Encina (Granada) had fractured nasal bones, and although this could easily have resulted from a domestic accident or fight another male skeleton found nearby had fractured ribs and a further female had a number of lesions to her body.

The skeletal evidence is far from conclusive and very little can be said about the nature and frequency of Bronze Age warfare from this evidence alone. There are examples where individuals have been injured and killed by arrowheads or by blows from sharp implements, and instances where limbs have been removed. Furthermore, there are a number of burials that deviate from the typical graves and funerary customs of the period – graves that may have been improvised. There are a number of possible explanations: these individuals may have been buried hastily, or perhaps their bodies could not be brought home for proper burial and a grave had to be improvised. Instances where bodies were buried or dumped in pits or ditches without grave-goods could represent the disposal of slain opponents, which explains why they did not receive the customary funerary ritual. They may also be the burials of the lower-status members of the group, the 'ordinary' warriors, since such burials are in strong contrast to the rich warrior burials of the emerging elite.

WEAPONS AND WARRIOR ACCOUTREMENTS

Weapons

Throughout the Neolithic and Copper Age the principal weapon, as far as we can discern, both for hunting and fighting, was the bow and arrow; this is confirmed by the presence of arrowheads found within fortified settlements and burials, lodged within skeletal remains and depicted in cave paintings. Other weapons must have existed although they were either made from perishable materials which have not survived, and/or cannot easily be identified owing to their multiple functions, for example sticks, clubs, stones (we can also include defensive tactics like the digging of pits and snares). The introduction or appearance of metalworking in the Copper Age brought no immediate changes or advantages in warfare and was largely used to make small, simple objects, such as hooks, knives, items of jewellery, simple daggers, plain axes and occasionally small arrowheads. The early use of metallurgy was more concerned with show, prestige and access to knowledge, than with practical improvements within farming, hunting or warfare. Metal production increased from the Final Copper Age/Beaker phase onwards and saw the introduction of new objects and weapons such as: 'Palmela' points (small metal points probably hafted to a wooden stake and used as a javelin), tongued points and new types of knives and daggers. The latter were attached to wooden or bone hilts. There were also improvements for archers with stone wristguards and more efficient arrowheads in stone, bone and occasionally metal. These changes represent clear evidence of a division between weapons used for hunting, and those used in warfare, and the deposition of these objects in burials reflects their increased symbolic and social properties.

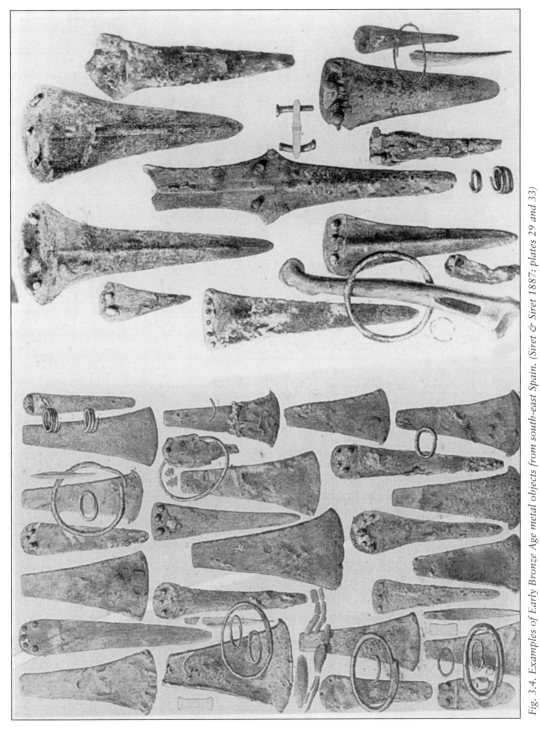

Fig. 3.4. Examples of Early Bronze Age metal objects from south-east Spain. (Siret & Siret 1887: plates 29 and 33)

Metal production continued to increase during the Early Bronze Age, although production was still at a low level, even at many of the major sites, and innovations were slow to spread across the peninsula. However, a new range of weapon types was now being produced, especially in the south-east, comprising halberds, classic forms of daggers and points, and larger numbers of metal arrowheads (**Fig. 3.4**) (Fernández Manzano & Montero Ruiz 1997). These may have been inspired or influenced by objects from beyond the Pyrenees although they are deemed to have been produced locally and not imported.

The introduction of new weapon types continued during the Middle Bronze Age with new forms of daggers and points, flat axes, swords, items of adornment, such as diadems, rings and pendants, and many more metal arrowheads. Daggers were becoming longer, while swords or rapiers became shorter. The appearance of silver metallurgy led to the production of silver-riveted daggers that would have had great symbolic value. Many metal objects ceased to be produced in the Late Bronze Age and the scale of metal production was significantly reduced with a general absence of personal ornamentation and displays of wealth. In the Final Bronze Age, the appearance of a range of 'Atlantic' bronze weapons, influenced by or direct imports from abroad, signified increased contact with other societies. A large inventory of offensive weapons, including heeled and looped axes and various types of swords, including the 'Carp's Tongue' sword, were introduced to Spain at this time from continental Europe. The distribution of these objects suggests uneven access to foreign trade and exchange, and many of these 'exotic' goods would have been used to support local elites.

The Early Bronze Age also sees the beginnings of funerary ritual involving the use of metal weapons and their deposition as grave-goods accompanying the deceased. The first evidence for votive deposits and the ritual destruction of weapons also appears at this time, confirming that social and ceremonial value was attached to these weapons. The extent to which such weapons were actually used prior to their deposition in graves or hoards has not been explored. Future research in the form of use-wear analysis is required to confirm whether these objects were produced primarily or exclusively for use as grave-goods, or whether they were the possessions of the deceased which they had used during their lifetime and which signified their social status and success as a warrior even in death. It is important to remember that these were not the first weapons to be deposited as grave-goods – arrowheads had been an important part of grave assemblages since the Neolithic period. Therefore it seems that it is the raw material that has changed rather than the object type or the funerary ritual itself. Being a relatively new technology, to which access and knowledge was restricted, metal objects would have assumed a great prestige value and would have been used as part of conspicuous consumption at feasts, funerals and other social gatherings and at funerals. Metal weapons are frequently depicted in rock carvings of the Bronze Age period and their recovery from stratified and datable contexts helps to date the rock art through the comparison of object types and forms (*see* pp. 59–60).

New types of weapon were adopted unevenly across the peninsula in the Bronze Age, with some areas continuing to use archaic types, while others adopted new weapons and the new styles of fighting associated with them. This unevenness is due to the nature and endurance of existing traditions and the degree of access to these new weapon types, knowledge of their production and/or influences from other groups. The adoption of new types of metal weapons meant a significant change in tactics although we have little direct (skeletal) evidence of the results of fighting. We see a dramatic shift from the Copper Age where fighting was carried out at long range, using speed and agility to outwit and out-manoeuvre the opponent(s), to close-combat fighting with, initially, much heavier and more cumbersome weapons. The daggers, swords, arrowheads and spear points evolved greatly towards the end of the Bronze Age, with improvements in metalworking technologies and more direct influences from other parts of Europe. Evidence from northern, western and central Europe (cited in Chapters Two and Four) illustrates that similar changes in weaponry taking place elsewhere were accompanied by an increase in forms of body protection, such as shields, helmets and armour. Although such evidence is generally lacking in the archaeological record of Spain, certainly until the end of the Bronze Age, the iconography suggests that similar trends may have taken place (see below).

Hoards/votive deposits

The first hoards involving the deposition of weapons in the ground are found in the Early Bronze Age. Votive deposition and the ritual destruction of weapons by depositing them in watery locations seems to begin in the Middle Bronze Age and reaches its maximum development in the later period. Where these are found at 'special' or strategic places such as important river-crossings, passes, hills or frontier areas they may imply the summoning of goodwill or luck from spirits and/or ancestors, perhaps in aiding success or affording protection to the group. Although we may never be sure of the real reason behind these deposits, 'these underwater finds may have had ritual value as a symbolic border between life and death, but also as a territorial border' (Ruíz-Gálvez Priego 1997: 113).

Examples of Bronze Age hoards and votive deposits can be found across the peninsula, with swords being the most common object. A number of weapons were recovered from the Guadalquivir River, including a Carp's Tongue sword, a ferrule and socketed spearheads. A small group of objects was found in the River Genil, including two Carp's Tongue swords, a small arrowhead and an unidentified bronze object, probably dating to the end of the Bronze Age period. More than 400 pieces of metalwork were found in the Huelva river, including Atlantic-type swords, spearheads, spear butts and daggers; these date to the end of the Bronze Age. Bronze hoards are frequently found in the south-west of Spain, and from *c.* 900 BC onwards they include Atlantic bronzes of non-local traditions. In contrast, few hoards are found in the north and north-east, certainly until the end of the Bronze Age, although this probably reflects the small amount of archaeological investigation that has taken place there.

Warrior's Panoply

Aside from weapons, very few parts of the warrior's panoply are found preserved in the archaeological record. Delicate objects, or those made from perishable materials such as wood and leather, do not tend to survive in the acidic soils and dry climatic conditions in Spain. Therefore we often have to rely on evidence from depictions in cave paintings and rock carvings in order to piece together rather disparate types of evidence (see below). Archaeological evidence for objects such as shields, though clearly represented on stelae, has not yet been found, and we can only assume that these would have been made from either wood or skins/leather. The same is true of bows and the bags or quivers that would have been used to hold arrows, and of any form of body protection that may have been used. One part of the warrior panoply that *is* found preserved in the archaeological record and is also seen in cave paintings and rock carvings is the helmet.

Helmets

Some forms of headgear, many reminiscent of antler horns or plumed hats, are found depicted in cave paintings of the Neolithic and Copper Age, as well as in the Bronze Age period. The only examples of actual helmets come from the Late Bronze Age or Early Iron Age and are few in number. The first is a bronze crested helmet found in a river in Huelva. Two large pieces are preserved from the main part, together with four fragments from the rim and four studs. The pieces form a conical-shaped helmet, with ribbing on the edge or rim and incised decorative lines towards the crest. According to some scholars, this type of helmet marks the arrival of Celtic invaders and of cultural influences from central and western Europe from the Final Bronze Age onwards. This helmet is tentatively dated to *c.* 750–700 BC. Similar crested helmets have been found elsewhere in Europe, for example at Armancourt (Oise, de Bernieres d'Ailly, Calvados), where they have been dated to the tenth, or early ninth century BC. In a deposit found at Larnaud (advanced Halstatt B), studs similar to those from Huelva were recovered. This type of object probably came to the Iberian peninsula via France along with other objects and influences from the first millennium BC onwards.

The second example comes from Cuevas de Vinromá, a mountainous area near the east coast (Almagro Gorbea 1973: 353–5, fig. 2). The helmet is relatively small, hemispherical and is decorated with a series of studs (**Fig. 3.5**). Rather unusually, this example is made of antler and silver, a metal not commonly used for helmets in Europe at this time. Similar examples of embossed decoration are found across Europe in the Late Bronze Age, providing a tentative date for this piece.

As discussed earlier, helmets are also depicted on rock carvings of the Bronze Age and earlier periods. Perhaps the most famous example comes from La Gasulla in Castellón (*see* **Fig. 3.8**). This shows a horse and mounted rider who wears a helmet with an angular crest. The helmet is very similar to the one from Huelva (discussed above) and some from Italy. Other examples come from stelae. Various different types of headgear are depicted, from the detailed to the highly schematic. Schematic types often have long antler horns (**Fig. 3.5**), which are generally attributed to a north European/Scandinavian origin. Another type is the helmet proper, which is usually conical in shape (as the Huelva example). Although examples of helmets are scarce in the archaeological record, this does not mean that they were not common in the Bronze Age, nor that they were unimportant. The extent to which these helmets were truly functional – as opposed to indicators of status or group affiliation (perhaps making individuals easily recognisable in the heat of a battle) – is not known. However, we can be fairly sure that the two examples found in

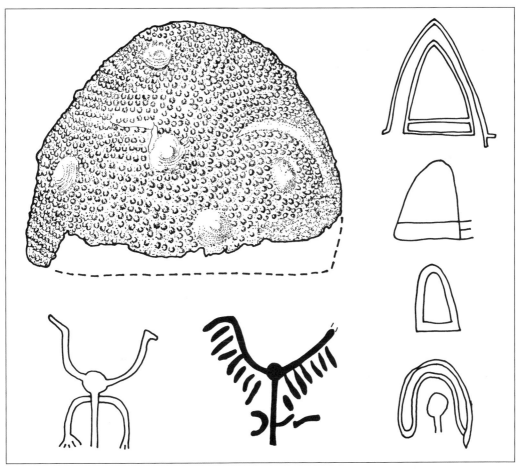

Fig. 3.5. The helmet from Cuevas de Vinromá (after Almagro Gorbea 1973: 353, fig. 2), and other examples taken from various stelae.

Spain would have afforded little actual protection for the head when being attacked by an arrow or receiving a blow from a sword.

Shields

No examples of shields have been found in the archaeological record as yet, but evidence from rock carvings suggests that they were part of the warrior's panoply. We must therefore assume that the main body of the shield would have been made of a perishable material, such as leather or wood, perhaps with metal or bone studs and other decorative elements. The shields represented in rock carvings all appear to be very similar (**Fig. 3.6**). All the recognisable examples are round, made up of concentric circles, often with a V-shaped wedge taken out of one side. This feature occurs on many Bronze Age shields, or depictions of shields, across much of Europe. In general, most of the Spanish depictions of

53

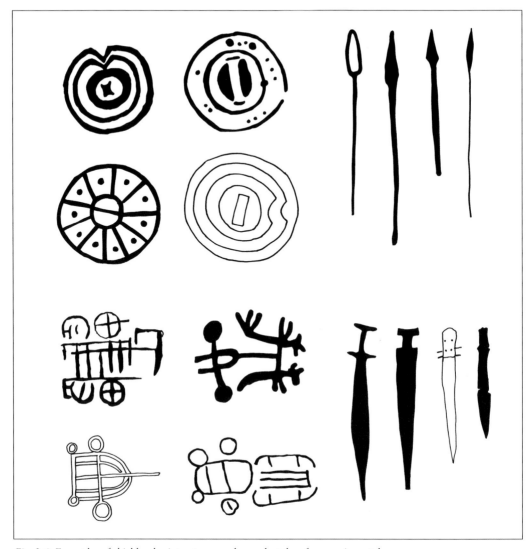

Fig. 3.6. Examples of shields, chariots, spears and swords, taken from various stelae.

shields have some type of motif in the centre (examples of which can be seen in **Fig. 3.6**), with small circles or dots, possibly representing studs. A small number have parallel lines across the entire shield, although these appear to be less common. The slight variations in the 'motifs' or central features of the shield, like the different styles of headgear, may be an indicator of social grouping.

Shields are not depicted alongside warriors in cave paintings of the Neolithic and Copper Age periods, and their introduction in the Bronze Age seems to coincide with the introduction of new weapons and the development of a new and different style of fighting which required body protection.

Chariots and horses

Images interpreted as wheeled vehicles, or chariots, are found among the schematic rock art of the peninsula, although they are far from common. The depictions are very similar and show two parallel lines or a box, with a series of lines running at right angles, and two circles on either side, usually with two lines crossing in the middle (**Fig. 3.6**). The chariots are viewed from above while the wheels and any animals are drawn from the side. Cuadrado places the earliest chariot depictions at *c.* 1000–900 BC (cited Acosta 1968: 104), although these dates almost certainly overlap with the beginning of the Iron Age.

Figure 3.7 shows a chariot pulled by two or more animals, depicted on a stela from Zarza Capilla (south-west Spain). The principal figure is a human figure with knee ornaments, and a sword hanging from his belt, a musical instrument (?), a shield, at least one mirror, a lance and a circular object (Vaquerizo Gil 1989). Another example, though much more schematic, comes from Zarza de Montanchez, Cáceres, where a four-wheeled chariot is pulled by two schematic animals. It could be argued that these 'wheeled vehicles' are in fact carts, perhaps pulled by oxen rather than horses, although their depiction alongside warriors and weapons does not fit with such a domestic and utilitarian interpretation. Furthermore, depictions of chariots are not very common and must surely denote a person of high status and considerable wealth. The appearance of chariots or wagons on stelae is again attributed to influences from elsewhere in Europe and is generally dated to the Late Bronze Age and Early Iron Age.

The first archaeological evidence for horse riding comes from the discovery of what appears to be part of a horse's harness from Fuente Alamo in Almería, *c.* 1300 BC (Fernández Manzano & Montero Ruiz 1997: 117). Circular metal disks, which have been interpreted in the same way, were found in a hoard at Llavorsi in Lerida, dating to the Final Bronze Age. Horses are seen in a few cave paintings, at Los Canforos (Peñarrubia) and Cueva de Doña Clotilde (Albarracin) and on stelae, although they are highly stylised and often difficult to distinguish from other types of animals. The earliest depiction of a mounted rider comes from Cingle de la Gasulla, Castellón, where the horse's mane and harness are clearly shown (**Fig. 3.8**). This scene is thought to date from around the eleventh to the twelfth century BC. Finally, at the Bronze Age site of Cerro de la Encina, a large assemblage of horse bones were found in an enclosure that has been argued to have some ritual significance, which strengthens the case for horses being an important status symbol at this time.

ICONOGRAPHY

In the Neolithic and Copper Age periods there existed cave paintings depicting warriors and/or hunters, animals, weapons, other schematic motifs, as well as scenes of fighting, dancing and hunting (**Fig. 3.9**). Often great attention was paid to detail with forms of dress and certain physical features being scrupulously portrayed. In some examples an attempt was made to distinguish warring groups through differences in the size of individuals, or through distinct physical features, or by showing figures with different types of headgear and head, leg or arm ornaments. The bow and arrow is by far the most

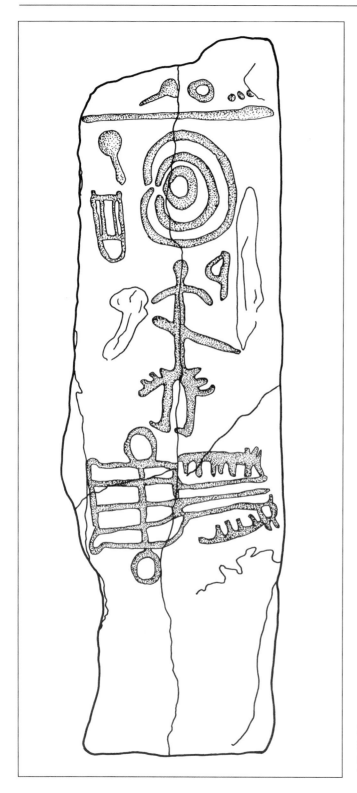

Fig. 3.7. Stela from Zarza Capilla,
Badajoz, showing a chariot drawn
by two or more animals. (After
Vaquerizo Gil 1989: 37)

Fig. 3.8. Mounted rider from Cingle de la Gasulla, Castellón. (After Ripoll Perelló 1966: 168, fig. 1)

Fig. 3.9. Cave painting from Cueva del Roure, Castellón, depicting warriors fighting. (After Beltran 1982: 44–5)

Fig. 3.10. Archers, dead and dying warriors from various Neolithic/Copper Age cave paintings. (After Beltrán 1982)

common weapon shown and bows are depicted in all stages of deployment in scenes of hunting and fighting. In some cases their size, relative to the figure(s), are exaggerated, presumably to enhance the symbolic message they contain. Other weapons include axes, swords, thrown projectiles, staffs and sticks/clubs. Although it can be difficult to distinguish between hunters and warriors when figures are depicted in isolation, there are a number of scenes that depict battles and gatherings of warriors. Dead or dying warriors are also depicted either with arrows sticking out of them or lying beneath archers with raised bows (**Fig. 3.10**).

Evidence for pre-Bronze Age warfare as seen through cave paintings shows a familiarity with 'the disposition and deployment of armed men' (Beltrán *et al.* 1986: 50) and the presence of some form of leadership denoted by different headgear and clothing. Scenes involving warriors and weapons deal with ethnic differentiation, real and symbolic battles, aggression and death. It should be noted that fighting appears to have been a male-dominated pursuit (sometimes confirmed by the presence of male genitalia), with females shown associated with activities such as dancing and gathering foodstuffs.

In the Bronze Age there seems to be a shift in the ways in which warriors and fighting were portrayed. Rock carvings and stelae show highly schematic anthropomorphic figures, different types of weapons, animals and other miscellaneous objects interpreted as mirrors, combs, musical instruments, shields and chariots (*see* **Fig. 3.7**). Unfortunately the stelae are rarely found in their original context and this has led to much speculation as to their function.

In the Bronze Age there are two main types of relief carvings and engravings which include weapons-stelae and carved rock surfaces. The earliest examples of decorated grave slabs or stelae are found in southern Portugal. These probably belong to the Early/Middle Bronze Age and appear to have been associated with cist burials, i.e. these slabs covered the burial and sealed the grave. The most common motifs found on them are halberds, swords, axes, bows and daggers. Although the stelae themselves do not look anthropomorphic in shape (i.e. the stone slabs do not appear to represent a human figure) straps are depicted linking the weapons, suggesting how they may have been arranged on the warrior (contrast with examples from Italy on pp. 107–11) (Jorge 1999b: 115). In general the associated burials do not seem to include the types of weapon shown and the depictions are more reminiscent of the rich Early Bronze Age burials of the south-east. This suggests that groups in other areas were depicting objects that were desired for their prestige value but were not necessarily attainable.

In the Late Bronze Age very few human figures are depicted on the stelae, making way for an array of objects: shields, lances, swords, helmets, bows, wagons, chariots, mirrors and combs. One of the most interesting observations about these stelae is that human figures are argued to have appeared at a time when more objects of a 'Mediterranean' type were in existence: 'The occurrence of a human figure (the "warrior") with the increasing representation of weapons and artefacts of Mediterranean origin, thus expressing the social standing of a leader in terms of his relation to long-distance trade with the Mediterranean world' (Jorge 1999b: 118).

It is not clear to what degree the groups of objects shown are commemorative or honorific, with the depictions reflecting either the deceased and their possessions, or objects symbolic of their former status and position in society. Judging by the wear and damage to many of the stelae, it would seem that they stood upright and exposed for some time, either when they were first erected or when put to a later use. Some of the stelae were found as covering slabs over graves, although it is likely that their significance goes beyond a purely functional interpretation. Indeed the stelae and their markings may have been used to mark social groupings, or ownership of territories and trade-routes.

One of the most detailed studies of Bronze Age rock carvings has been carried out in the region of Galicia in north-west Spain. Here, weapons are not as common as animals and abstract motifs, although they do exist, and the repertoire of weapons is limited to daggers and halberds (**Fig. 3.11**). Sometimes a large number of weapons are shown in a variety of sizes on one stone and it has been argued that the arrangement of motifs may have some formality, possibly echoing hoards. The rock carvings found at Leiro, for example, consisted of both halberds and daggers and were located not far from a hoard containing similar objects. The weapon carvings of Galicia show a preference for high places, located on the edges of estuaries and rivers, or locations with extensive views, possibly controlling routes of communication. 'Like the antlers of the stags, they present an image of male aggressiveness and could have supported similar claims to territory and position' (Bradley 1997: 207). The Galician examples appear to share a number of features with the

Fig. 3.11. Weapons engraved on a rock from Galicia. (Photo: Richard Bradley)

composition of hoards or votive deposits found in other parts of Europe (Bradley 1997: 250–1). Galician weapon carvings seem to appear at a time when no artificially defended sites are known in the area and the actual warriors are hardly ever shown; only a small group of weapon carvings show anthropomorphic figures, sometimes accompanied by a single weapon. 'The anthropomorphs, . . . in northern Iberia were associated with individual weapons, usually daggers, while the artefacts depicted on the cist slabs of Alentejo appear to represent single sets of artefacts in which no items are duplicated in the same composition' (Bradley 1997: 247).

By the Late Bronze Age most carvings showing weapons had disappeared from Galicia, although more weapons are found in hoards and as grave-goods. 'The ritual importance of weaponry remained as strong as it had been, but more of these objects entered the archaeological record' (Bradley 1997: 251). This was contemporary with the first signs of defended settlements and a highly structured society led by a warlike elite.

CONCLUSIONS

The location of Copper Age sites was determined first and foremost by economic and logistical factors, therefore access to vital resources – water and good cultivable land – was paramount. The availability of naturally defended locations was a secondary, though not unimportant, factor. The artificially defended sites were very much geared towards the use of archery, with archers shielded by high protective walls, bastions and towers, often with small arrow-slits, and probably the use of timber superstructures from which to observe the enemy and launch counter-attacks. Attempts to defend sites took the form of perimeter walls enclosing all or part of the occupied area. In a small number of cases this became very sophisticated, for example at Los Millares in the south-east. In the majority of cases the defences can be seen to evolve through time rather than following an organised, planned defensive scheme. Defensive ditches are only rarely found, principally because most sites tended to be located on rock outcrops, and in the case of low-lying sites on plains and in river valleys, evidence for outlying ditches, now silted up, has not been sought. Evidence for the use of timber structures is rarely encountered, except where post-holes are found adjacent to walls or in the case of Cerro de la Virgen (Granada) where timber posts were found embedded in the defensive walls, presumably forming the foundation for an upper structure.

Evidence from cave paintings, from skeletal remains and weapons supports the idea that warfare was present, possibly even prevalent, in Copper Age society, and was based largely on archery. It is clear that attempts had been made to increase the efficiency of weapons and to protect settlements and their inhabitants, and that many of the objects associated with warfare had begun to assume greater symbolic properties both for the living and the dead.

In the Bronze Age changes in the location, layout and organisation of settlements can be attributed to changes in the social and political organisation of groups. A high degree of planning and strategy is evident from the outset. Fortification walls were built where natural defence was lacking, while the selection of easily defensible locations meant that energy, time and raw material investment was kept to a minimum. The construction of domestic houses on terraces, inter-locked through passages and stairways, was an efficient and effective way of coping with limited domestic space and providing defence at the same time. The location of sites and their defences would imply that the tactics of warfare had changed. Such sites would have been very difficult to attack. Siege tactics, literally surrounding the site and starving those inside or burning the site, would perhaps have been the only effective means of defeating a rival group. Some of the sites were built around or encompassed a natural spring which must have been vital in such instances. Water conservation has long been argued to be an important aspect of Bronze Age sites in the south-east. Evidence for this comes from cisterns located within or immediately outside settlements, for example at the sites of El Oficio, Fuente Alamo and Gatas, all in Almería (Chapman 1990: 125–7). Evidence for burning is found at a number of sites, but attributing this to warfare rather than to domestic accidents (especially considering the metallurgical activities taking place at many of these sites) is very difficult.

An alternative tactic to siege warfare would be to attack members of the group away from the site – hunting and fishing parties, those working in the fields or tending animals. This may partly explain why we find relatively few weapons, especially arrowheads, within and around settlement defences at this time. Furthermore, there are no ditches to 'collect' and preserve evidence for the use of spears and arrowheads in attacking sites. If groups were attacked away from the main site we are unlikely to find much evidence for fighting. It is also clear from the burial record that not all levels of society were receiving burial in an archaeologically visible form at this time and more often than not we have only the graves of the elite, and not necessarily those directly involved in fighting. This greatly skews our picture of the ordinary warrior and creates problems in generalising about exactly who was fighting, with what weapons and how they were buried and commemorated. This problem is echoed on the rock carvings and grave stelae where it is difficult to judge precisely how representative the warrior's panoply depicted actually is. It seems likely that these are representations of elite warriors and a set of prestige goods that had a social, symbolic and perhaps largely non-functional meaning. Although the stelae depict parts of the panoply that do not survive in the archaeological record, we do not know the extent to which all warriors had these forms of body protection and accoutrements. The weapon hoards reflect the enormous symbolism attached to warfare, and the location of such hoards and rock carvings appears deliberate and meaningful in ways that we can only surmise.

Essentially the major differences in the nature of warfare from the Copper Age to the Bronze Age were an increase in the organisation and efficiency of sites and their defences, partly the result of a stronger central authority (the elite), and the need for the efficient storage and protection of important resources, stored food surpluses and craft objects. The notable increase in the symbolism attached to weapon and warrior paraphernalia is evident in the burials, hoards and artistic representations of the period. Major changes in the types of weapons used meant new tactics in fighting: a shift from warfare largely based on archery and other projectiles thrown by mobile warriors, to close-combat fighting with heavier cutting and thrusting weapons and requiring some form of body protection (**Fig. 3.12**). It seems clear that in much of the evidence we are seeing a picture of the elite warrior becoming less involved in the actual fighting but surrounded with objects conveying status and power. Evidence for the ordinary warrior becomes less apparent and it may be that the advent of the Bronze Age brought very few changes to the ways in which men fought, other than changes in authority and the motivation for fighting.

The motives behind fighting in the Bronze Age are likely to be many and varied. The location of defended sites close to important resources and natural routes of communication suggests that competition and conflict may have arisen over access to these and to the trade in raw materials and finished goods. The importance of metal

Fig. 3.12. Reconstruction of a Late Bronze Age warrior from Spain. (Simon Pressey)

became paramount as the Bronze Age began, especially for the elite who used metal objects to symbolise their power and authority and to provide them with tradable goods.

Contact and exchange with groups beyond the Iberian peninsula at the end of the Bronze Age and in the Early Iron Age had far-reaching effects on existing traditions, leading to the fragmentation and disruption of local patterns of trade, socio-political links and systems of authority. Settlements lost their organisational qualities and became less structured units, new sites occupied less defensive positions and there was generally less investment in defences, except where mining was taking place. The influx of foreigners (most probably attracted by Spain's rich mineral resources), new ideas and new technologies brought far-reaching changes to all aspects of Bronze Age society and saw the first foreign colonies established on the southern coast of Spain.

FURTHER READING

Bradley, R. 1997. *Rock Art in the Prehistory of Atlantic Europe* (Routledge)

Chapman, R. 1990. *Emerging Complexity: The later prehistory of south-east Spain, Iberia and the west Mediterranean* (Cambridge University Press)

Harrison, R.J. 1994. 'The Bronze Age in Northern and North-eastern Spain 2000–800 BC', in C. Mathers & S. Stoddart (eds), *Development and Decline in the Mediterranean Bronze Age* (Sheffield Archaeological Monographs 8, J.R. Collis), pp. 73–98

Jorge, S. Oliveira, 1999a. 'Bronze Age Settlements and Territories on the Iberian Peninsula: New considerations', in K. Demakopoulou, C. Eluère, J. Jensen, A. Jockenhövel & J.-P. Mohen (eds), *Gods and Heroes of the European Bronze Age* (Thames and Hudson), pp. 60–4

Jorge, S. Oliveira. 1999b. 'Bronze Age Stelae and Menhirs of the Iberian Peninsula: Discourses of power', in K. Demakopoulou, C. Eluère, J. Jensen, A. Jockenhövel & J.-P. Mohen (eds), *Gods and Heroes of the European Bronze Age* (Thames & Hudson), pp. 114–22

Mathers, C. 1994. 'Goodbye to All That? Contrasting Patterns of Change in the South-East Iberian Bronze Age c. 24/2200–600 BC', C. Mathers & S. Stoddart (eds), *Development and Decline in the Mediterranean Bronze Age* (Sheffield Archaeological Monographs 8, J.R. Collis), pp. 21–72

FOUR

CENTRAL AND EASTERN EUROPE

INTRODUCTION

The area defined as central and eastern Europe will draw in examples from Germany, Switzerland, Austria, Hungary, Slovakia, the Czech Republic, Poland, Bulgaria and Russia. This is the largest region covered by a single chapter and much of what we think of as representing the 'Bronze Age' was integral to this area. Trade connected the northern and western regions of Europe (*see* Chapter Two) to this area and innovations in goods, weapons and settlements often originated here. Some elements clearly differ between specific regions but it is possible to tease out general trends. Warfare was certainly an important part of the lives of Bronze Age inhabitants of central and eastern Europe and this is reflected in much of the archaeological evidence available.

As in the preceding chapters, numerous elements of the evidence support the argument for the presence of conflict. Bronze Age settlements have been known for many years, and their role in trade and the reasons for their specific location are increasingly understood. In numerous cases sites were provided with defences, either against animals or the elements, or against attack, culminating in the great defended sites of the Urnfield period. Burials, too, hint at the importance of warrior status and some bodies even display wounds suffered in raids or battle, while the weapons used to inflict the wounds are found in relative abundance not only as stray finds but also in hoards and burials. The panoply of arms changed over time and with it the types of combat. Taken together, all the strands of information tie together to give a convincing picture of the nature of warfare in the Bronze Age of central and eastern Europe.

SETTLEMENTS AND FORTIFICATIONS

The provision of defences around certain dwellings or locations seems to hint at times of stress. In much of central and eastern Europe archaeological traces of early settlement sites are rare; where they are visible, they are often very simple. From the start of the Bronze Age many settlements were located at important points on trade-routes, especially on rivers or trans-isthmian passes. These points eventually became important enough to be subjected to raids, but rather than abandoning them the inhabitants chose to deal with the problem by fortifying the sites.

At the dawn of the Bronze Age agrarian activities were of prime importance to social groups. At Pustynka in Poland, for example, there were a number of rectangular houses seemingly accompanied by buildings with an agricultural function. Settlements were generally small scale and comprised disparate communities (Coles & Harding 1979: 122). In the Tisza basin and along the Danube Early Bronze Age sites took the form of tells or nucleated villages. Artificial barriers were sometimes built around early sites, often with ditches and banks surrounding them, as at the tell of Tószeg, which was on an important trade-route. Some settlements made use of naturally defensible positions, for example, at Wietenberg in Romania the site was placed on a high plateau. Excavation of this Höhensiedlung (hill settlement) also revealed evidence of domestic occupation in the form of many pits and a hearth. Other hill sites of Wietenberg type have been found, typically located on medium-sized hills or beside rivers. As these were in naturally defensible locations, fortifications have not been added.

In contrast, settlement sites from the Early Bronze Age that were not in naturally defensible locations were sometimes provided with banks and ditches. This seems to have been an important feature both in the Late Únětice Culture of east Germany, and also in the Otomani settlements of Romania. A number of the tell settlements seem to have been burned and abandoned towards the end of the Early Bronze Age, which may point towards attacks and a genuine need for protection. It will always be difficult to understand the relationship between fortified and non-fortified sites (and, in the later period, the hillforts). Were people occupying one sort of settlement and utilising the other only at times of conflict, or were they totally independent entities?

The Late Bronze Age or Urnfield Period in this region was still largely one of small-scale settlements, many of which were sited along major river valleys, on lake-shores or on hills. For example, in Germany there were habitation locations along the Rhine, Moselle and Main river valleys. Switzerland retains a great deal of well-preserved evidence of Late Bronze Age settlement with extensive dwellings around Lakes Neuchâtel and Léman. Here remains were found of the so-called 'pile-dwellings' (houses on stilt-like platforms) as well as evidence for pottery industries, textiles and agriculture. Though the lakeside settlements may have been abandoned quite rapidly, there was no evidence for attacks on these sites.

In addition to the sites involved with the production of goods such as textiles or with agriculture, many settlements were connected to the trade in prestige goods and as a result may have come under frequent attack. Copper and salt were vital resources, the former for the manufacture of bronze, the latter as a basic necessity of human life. Sites thus developed in areas with access to these commodities. In Austria, for example, settlements near Salzburg were producing copper, while at Hallstatt, the famous type-site for the Early Iron Age, and at Dürrnberg bei Hallein in the Salzkammergut there is evidence for Bronze Age salt production (though the latter is especially noted for its Iron Age workings). In addition, it has been noted in the archaeological literature that settlements were placed near another human necessity – water.

By the end of the Bronze Age much of the domestic activity and production of goods seems to have taken place at fortified sites. Our picture of the Late Bronze Age has been distorted by the destruction of much of the archaeological evidence, but nevertheless this does seem to indicate that the need for defence was strong. Sites of the Urnfield period were occasionally situated in areas where no prior settlement had existed and often in locations that would not be reoccupied for a further thousand years. Was this indicative of the great pressure on land possibly caused in part by deterioration in the climate? If so, this could have been a major cause of disagreement – and thus a possible motive for violence.

As with western and northern Europe, the Urnfield Period of this region sees the emergence of a new type of settlement – the hillfort. These sites were generally located on higher ground and often provided with formidable defences. If bronze weapons were the ultimate symbols of power for the Bronze Age warrior, then the hillforts represent the zenith of Bronze Age defensive technologies. Much excavation work remains to be done on fortified sites of the Bronze Age before we have a comprehensive overall picture as few such sites have been investigated on a large scale and it is rare for intensive excavations to have been undertaken. Although the Urnfield Period of the Late Bronze Age saw the rise of true fortified sites on a large scale throughout the region, some earlier defended sites have been found, certainly they seem to have appeared earlier than those of western and northern Europe. Some authors have tried to distinguish different phases of fortification construction in central Europe and three main ones seem to have been teased out: the first during the transition between the Early and Middle Bronze Age, the second at the start of the Late Bronze Age, and the third at the very end of the Bronze Age. Fortification was rare in the Tumulus Cultures of the region, and the few sites were generally small in scale, enclosing up to around 3ha (Jockenhövel 1999).

The early sites that have been examined by archaeologists include the agrarian settlement at Spišsky Štvrtok in Slovakia. This site has revealed traces of a large stone fortification wall – which still stands up to 1m high – and a rampart some 7m thick in places. In addition, round tower bastions may have protected part of the defences. The site was ideally placed to dominate a pass northwards through the Carpathians to the Upper Vistula in Poland. Gold and bronze objects have been found in deposits within the enclosed 6000m² of Spišsky Štvrtok, perhaps indicating its importance in connection with the trade-routes (Coles & Harding 1979: 77).

Another Slovakian site frequently cited in the archaeological literature is Zámeček at Nitriansky Hradok (**Fig. 4.1**), close to the River Nitra. At around 1800BC this Bronze Age settlement was surrounded by a timber-framed rampart and a double ditch; the outer ditch was V-shaped and very large, being some 4.5m deep and around 10m wide. This site was linked to the trade network along the River Nitra and yielded a bronze hoard of five axes and a spearhead alongside finds of decorated bonework. One more Slovakian site is worthy of mention. Barca had substantial occupation deposits, around 2.5m deep, with many houses laid out in a grid and enclosed with a circular ditch and bank. The late occupation material included many ornaments and objects, such as a bronze dagger, an amber necklace and gold hair rings, and seemed to indicate destruction of the site by fire. However, it should be noted that burning does not necessarily equate with violent attack, as many examples of accidental destruction of settlements by fire are known from both archaeology and history.

Many Early Bronze Age sites in the Carpathian Basin seemed to require the construction of defences. Perhaps hinting at a regional centralised hierarchy, fortified settlements were also present in low-lying areas along river valleys, where they were susceptible to periodic flooding. It is possible that the barriers at these sites may have been used more as flood defences than as deterrents against attack. It must be said, though, that the network of

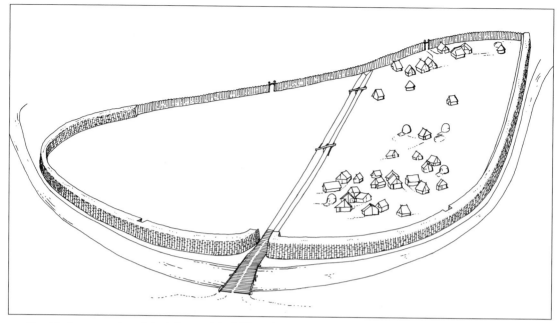

Fig. 4.1. Reconstruction of the defences of the hillfort of Nitriansky Hradok in Slovakia. (After Jockenhövel 1999)

ditches and banks around these sites would have provided a significant barrier against any would-be attacker.

Other early sites were constructed to dominate passes or trade-routes. At the Cetǎçuia (citadel) of Otomani, overlooking the great Hungarian plain, there were a number of fairly substantial defences despite the fact that the total area enclosed was small. The defences consisted of a rampart, a possible palisade and a V-shaped enclosure ditch. Clearly major defensive elements were being constructed throughout much of the region at an early stage in the Bronze Age; this situation continued in the Middle Bronze Age and exploded in the Late Bronze Age (Coles & Harding 1979: 75).

A Middle Bronze Age site known as 'Skalka' at Velim in Bohemia was equipped with ramparts, palisades and a series of ditches for defence. Excavators believed that these defences were ultimately destroyed by a heavy fire which was the result of an attack. The bronze arrowheads excavated in association with this destruction provided the main justification for this theory. Wooden posts, part of the rampart structure, fell into the ditch and were then buried by stones which fell from the collapsed rampart (Hrala *et al.* 1992). A number of bodies were found in association with this destruction level, though as much of the site seems to have been connected with votive practices, including intriguing burial rites, this cannot be cited as definitive proof of an attack. The Hohlandsberg in Alsace is another site that seems to contain much Middle Bronze Age material; this site was on high ground and dominated the Rhine valley below.

The construction of substantial defences really took off across almost the entire region in the Urnfield Period – in some cases they enclosed large areas, up to around 30ha, but substantial systematic excavation is still lacking and thus we cannot be too dogmatic about specific functions for individual sites. What does seem probable, however, is that their construction was connected not only to increasing competition over the trade-routes but also to the division of the landscape into territories. Individual sites were constructed to protect trade routes and to produce tradable items – metalwork, textiles, pottery and suchlike – while others were more closely associated with a ritual usage or perhaps simply to enhance the prestige of the elite.

The best-known sites are located in the Rhine-Main Basin in Germany, and in the Lausitz region of eastern Germany and Poland. In Lausitz five distinct types of fortification have been distinguished: two variants of plank-and-palisade type, a box type, a grid type and a drystone wall type. These Lusatian types may be linked to particular territories and some seem to have been rapidly ruined, with destruction layers visible in archaeological excavations. Biskupin in Poland is just such a site. Although most of the evidence here dates from the Iron Age, it was almost certainly extensively occupied in the Bronze Age and had timber defences. Izdebno, again in Poland, was also fortified, and many of its defensive timbers have been preserved in the bordering lake (A. Pidyn pers. comm.). A further Lausitz site, Nieder-Neundorf, used timbers to make an almost solid wooden rampart.

The majority of the fortified sites of the Rhine-Main region seem to be dated firmly to the Urnfield Period. Großer Stiefel in the Saarland has yielded tenth-century material from excavations and the Schwanburg seems datable at least to the tenth or ninth centuries. Urnfield datable material was also recovered from the promontory forts of Lemberg near Stuttgart and Dreifaltigkeitsberg. Ipf too had a number of Urnfield Period finds as did the Gelbe Bürg in Bavaria. As one might expect, the defences of these German sites varied in type. Drystone walls, earthen walls and timber box-structures were all employed as barriers against attack.

Many of the fortified sites in the Main valley are found on hills up to 300m above sea level, and most were positioned on promontories. This meant that they really needed only one rampart to protect the settlement, the steep hillsides effectively protecting the other sides. Fortifications were also added to low-lying sites. The Wasserburg near Bad Buchau in Germany was a fortified island (80m x 90m) of the Urnfield Period. This island had palisades with entrances guarded by large wooden towers (*see* Härke 1979).

Cezavy Hill near Blučina in Moravia was fortified from the late Únetice Culture and contained many Late Bronze Age burials. These have been interpreted as the burials of defenders slaughtered during an attack on the site. If so, this is one of the few examples of a Bronze Age fortified site which offers evidence for an attack. The Lausitz site of Sobiejuchy in Poland also had burned levels associated with arrowheads and human remains. Although this evidence may date to the Early Iron Age, it indicates that such sites still retained an important martial function (Bukowski 1962).

What were the fortified sites for? Some were a part of a network of settlements, many of which were undefended, with the hillfort providing protection to the inhabitants of all the sites during periods of unrest. Other sites would have been settlement units in their own right, while others played a role in the protection of trade-routes. This latter group includes those earlier sites of Slovakia that lay on the trade-routes in the Carpathians involving prestige goods such as amber.

Evidence for both hoards and metal-working has been found at many of the fortified sites – Großer Knetzberg had both, as did Hesselberg. The control of metal exploitation was of vital importance to those at the head of hierarchies. The central European region was of particular importance because north–south trading traffic had to cross it. Goods had to pass through the region en route from Scandinavia to Italy and vice-versa. Communities in the region could intensify the production of local goods and off-load them on the traders who passed through.

As in other parts of Europe, the fact that land was such an important element in Late Bronze Age life made the protection of societies and land vital. As the amount of land available for cultivation dwindled, it is likely that competition for it increased, leading to raiding, partly reflected perhaps by the increase in weaponry. The development of hillforts and other defended sites in central and eastern Europe was probably an attempt to counter this and, although definite examples of attacks on these sites are extremely rare, their very existence indicates the necessity for a degree of protection and suggests that social groups felt vulnerable to attack. But these sites were not simply constructed for defence – they also performed other functions, such as displaying the power and prestige of those responsible for their construction. In addition, archaeologists are increasingly assigning a votive role for these sites.

If the warrior was important in the Bronze Age, then so was the defended site, as a response to raids. What then of the individuals who lived in central and eastern Europe in the Bronze Age? Can the burial practices or the individuals themselves tell us anything about conflict?

BURIALS AND PALAEOPATHOLOGY

It is not easy to make bold statements about Bronze Age societies based solely on the methods they employed to dispose of their dead. Rather than being a direct reflection of contemporary society, burials and cremations with grave-goods were a statement of how people wanted the dead, their ancestors, to be perceived by their own and perhaps future societies. Nevertheless we can obtain useful nuggets of information pertaining to warriors and conflict in the Bronze Age from the archaeology of death.

As one would expect, burial traditions certainly varied over time and in different areas. A general survey is sufficient here to in provide an understanding of the period and to illustrate the various weapons used in rituals for the dead. In the transition from the Neolithic to the Bronze Age, dramatic depositions are found, often portraying the dead as rich, powerful warriors. Perhaps the most spectacular burial comes from Varna in Bulgaria where the astonishing Copper Age tomb of a 45-year-old man held around 990 individual objects of gold alongside flint tools and copper weapons including an axe and a projectile head. In addition, weaponry is found in a number of graves of the pre-Únětice cultures in Slovakia, including the so-called Nitra groups, which included burials with copper bracelets and flint arrowheads among other things.

In the Early Bronze Age, much of central Europe was under the influence of the Únětice Cultures. Initially the dead seem to have been disposed of in flat burials, without any covering barrows. The inhumed corpse might be accompanied by weaponry such as daggers or arrowheads and wristguards (similar indeed to the Beaker package described in Chapter Two). In addition to this group there were, 'Corded Ware' groups in eastern and central Europe using inhumations accompanied by a stone battle-axe and a corded ware beaker. Some of these flat burials occurred in large cemeteries, including the site of Únětice itself in the Czech Republic, which had approximately sixty inhumations, and Dolní Počernice, which had around seventy-seven graves (Coles & Harding 1979: 38). In the later Únětice period burial methods included interments in storage jars ('pithoi') and in wooden coffins. Throughout the period such graves sometimes seem to contain weaponry such as daggers and flanged axes, while some sites in Poland also produce halberds.

Other regions of eastern Europe also reveal traces of the weaponry of the period, illustrating its importance. Roughly contemporary with the late Corded Ware groups to the north and with the Únětice Culture groups to the north-west, the Catacomb Cultures of the Ukraine utilised barrow burials with timber-lined chambers. These, too, held the axes and arrowheads of the Early Bronze Age as well as flint daggers. (A series of carved figures from this period also depicts this weaponry, *see* pp. 83–5.)

Like those of the Catacomb Cultures, the great Early Bronze Age burial mounds in central Germany (also known as 'princely burials') made use of a wooden mortuary structure over which an earthen mound was heaped. At Leubingen a barrow some 34m in diameter was constructed to cover a timber mortuary structure within which lay the remains of an old man accompanied by a younger individual. The old man was given a great deal of weaponry for his passage to the afterlife – a halberd, three daggers and two axes – as well as a globular pot and much gold. Similarly, at Helmsdorf another 34m-diameter mound covered a wooden structure containing the inhumation of a man who had been buried with a flat bronze axe, a dagger, a hammer and a pot (Coles & Harding, 1979: fig. 13). At Łęki Małe in Poland the grave under the smallest burial mound in a group of eleven, was found to be similarly furnished. Here, the primary burial of a male had been given a dagger, an axe and a bronze pin. A female burial was also found in this mound, as was a secondary male burial (Demakopoulou *et al.* 1999: 255).

Hungary was perhaps rather unusual in terms of Early Bronze Age burial traditions in having a mixture of cremations and burials, as in the Nagyrév cemeteries of Toszeg-Ökörhalom. Some of the urns here were covered with bowls. Other burial practices in Hungary included the inhumation cemetery of Hernádkak, where one skeleton displays a classic combat wound (see below).

The post-Únětician Period also adopted burials under barrows and this epoch across much of central Europe has become known as the Hügelgräberbronzezeit – the Tumulus Culture. The burial rituals of this group showed much uniformity across large tracts of central Europe, although, of course, exceptions did exist such as Dolny Peter in Slovakia where both cremations and inhumations were found.

At the height of the Tumulus Culture we find the appearance of swords within graves. The so-called royal grave at Keszthely near Lake Balaton, Hungary, contained an inhumation with a pot, pin and a sword of Keszthely type. This burial was found in a stone chamber. Under a barrow in the south Bohemian cemetery at Houštka was an inhumation with a bronze flange-hilted sword. In addition, bronze arrowheads were found – archery persisted strongly in the Middle Bronze Age burial record and was seemingly deemed important as an expression of martiality. Velim, another Bohemian site of the Middle Bronze Age, contained numerous inhumations, many of which were found in ditches or near the ditched edges of the site, and their nature suggests that they were part of some ritual practice other than straightforward burial of the deceased (Hrala *et al.* 1992). Some possible evidence for violence is also seen on the bodies from this site.

German burials towards the end of the Middle Bronze Age (around 1300 BC) also contained arrowheads. At Hagenau near Regenstauf there was an inhumation under a tumulus with very rich grave-goods. Aligned north–south, the body was found to have both a long and a short flange-hilted sword, a flange-hilted dagger, an axe, four socketed arrowheads, a stone blade and other rich finds. Forty-three decorative pins were also discovered beneath a pottery vessel and have been interpreted as the studs of a now-decayed wooden shield. Not surprisingly, given the emphasis on arms in this grave, the burial has often been referred to as that of a Middle Bronze Age chieftain or warrior (Boos 1999: 106–7).

In general terms the Late Bronze Age of central and eastern Europe is defined at least in part by a significant shift in burial practices, from inhumations, often under barrows, to cremations. This surely represents a significant change in attitudes to the dead, perhaps reflecting the increased importance of the ancestors in relation to the emergence of tribal identity, linked to division of the land and competition between distinct groups? If so, this could be a powerful motive for conflict.

In central Europe there are many cemeteries with cremations, notably the Lausitz groups of Poland. For example, at Kraśnik, Lublin, there were around 400 cremations, mostly in urns, and at Malá Bělá there were 181. Some cremations from this period are also found in cists. These great urn cemeteries are found in much of Germany as well, some near pre-existing barrows such as at Morsum, and they also tend to dominate in Hungary and Yugoslavia, with examples at Csabrendek and Gáva. Of course there were exceptions: 727 inhumed bodies were found at Przeczyce in Lower Silesia alongside Late Bronze Age grave-goods, while in Bohemia the cemetery of Mladá Boleslav-Čejetičky contains tumuli of Únětice, Tumulus, Lausitz and Hallstatt periods (Plesl 1961: 40, 67 and 236). That arrowheads still existed in the Late Bronze Age is further shown by a rich grave at Wollmesheim near Rheinland-Pfalz in Germany. This probable double-inhumation contained a flange-hilted sword, decorative bronzes, and tanged and socketed arrowheads.

In the Late Bronze Age one also finds elements of wagons (or at least hints at their existence). One grave at Liegau-Augustusbad in Germany held much material along with the remains of a man who may well have been an important individual in life. Included in his burial assemblage were a metal vessel and a miniature wagon. The wagon grave at Hart an der Alz in Bavaria held a bronze sword, wagon-fittings, including bird-shaped mountings, and bronze vessels. Interestingly bronze arrowheads were also found here (Müller-Karpe 1959: 156).

At this stage we have reached the ultimate portrayal of the warrior in Bronze Age societies, equipped with exquisite bronze weaponry, the result of complex and highly skilled metal-working techniques, and with wagons and elements of feasting gear all connected to elaborate ceremonies and display. Burial practices throughout the region varied over time, and certainly regional traditions began to break away from the standard typological divisions of Tumulus Culture and Urnfield Culture. None the less weaponry is found in many disparate types of funerary context and was certainly deemed important as an expression of the nature of the deceased and/or their wealth. Daggers, arrowheads and axes were the dominant forms of weaponry in the earlier burial groupings while, in the later part of the Bronze Age swords are also found buried with the deceased.

The study of the dead is perhaps more revealing in attempting to prove the occurrence of combat. Trauma to human skeletons may indicate the actual use of the weapons so readily provided for the deceased in burial rites. Although there are not many examples, weapons injuries have been found on skeletons of pre-Bronze Age origin. An Eneolithic body from Jelšovce in Slovakia displayed a classic spear-piercing wound to the pelvis. Weapons trauma was thus not a new thing in the Bronze Age and there are a number of human skeletons that show weapons injuries. Projectile wounds are the norm, although this is perhaps more indicative of the weapons injuries that are most easily recognised and survive best in the archaeological record, rather than a true representation of dominant combat types. Instances of weapons trauma have been found on sites of the Tumulus Culture and also of Urnfield date across the study region and, although we cannot examine all the excavated examples here, those listed are intended to represent a broad cross-section.

Cremations are fairly common in Early Bronze Age Hungary, but the site of Hernádkak also contained a large quantity of inhumations. Graves 39, 96 and 122 produced bronze spearheads, daggers and flat axes, while grave 111 contained three boar's tusks. The skeleton in grave 122, like the bodies from Tormarton and Dorchester-on-Thames discussed in Chapter Two, had been pierced by a bronze spearhead. This weapon had transfixed the pelvis of the victim and was retained in death (**Fig. 4.2**). Seemingly this man had suffered a violent attack, the testament to which he took to his grave (Bóna 1975: 150 and Tafel 155).

Other projectile wounds were suffered by Tumulus Culture peoples in central Europe. A skeleton from Klings in Germany had a bronze arrowhead embedded in a vertebra (**Fig. 4.3**). Shot into the body from behind, the arrowhead would have resulted in immediate paralysis but not death. It has been assumed that further flesh-wounds were received which killed the victim (Feustel 1958: 8). A body at Stetten near Karlstadt in Germany had suffered a gruesome arm injury. Upon excavation of the grave, the skeleton was seen to have an arrowhead jutting out of its humerus. The grave also contained a bronze pin of a type found in the Tumulus Culture (Fröhlich 1983: 41). Vital parts of this skeleton were missing and it has thus proved difficult to be certain about the exact cause of death. It does, however, seem reasonable to believe that he may have been killed in an attack, one element of which was still archaeologically visible in his body.

The famous fortified hilltop settlement known as Skalka at Velim in eastern Bohemia contains several fascinating Middle/Late Bronze Age inhumations. The excavators believed this site had been abandoned after a violent destruction, as many bodies were buried together in the ditches and pits of the settlement. A number of them were found with prestige objects such as gold wire, bracelets and pins and it is possible that the majority, if not all, of these bodies related to a ritual act associated with the dead as opposed to out-and-out violence. Human sacrifice has been suggested as one explanation for the large

Fig. 4.2. The human skeletal remains from Grave 122 at Hernádkak, Hungary, with a spear embedded in the pelvis. (Photo: Magyar Nemzeti Múzeum)

numbers of people in these ditches and the cracks on several bones has raised the possibility of cannibalism, with the bones being split to obtain the marrow (Harding 1999: 158).

In addition to these burials, and some that had been inhumed in a more regular manner, one skeleton was thought to be a possible victim of the attack that destroyed the rampart at Velim. The body was located at the bottom of the site's latest fortification ditch and was associated with traces of fire and stones from the destroyed rampart structure (Hrala *et al.* 1992: 302). A number of other bodies here also suffered wounds and conflict may have been the cause of several deaths.

The fascinating settlement site of Cezavy Hill, Blučina, in Moravia, held many burials of the Late Bronze Age Velatice Culture. Initially the remains of 205 individuals found here

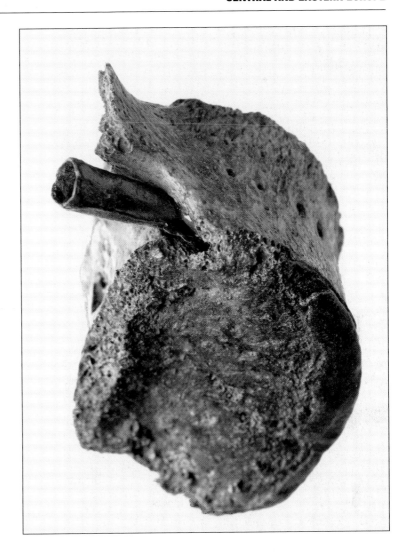

Fig. 4.3. Human vertebra with a bronze arrowhead embedded within it, from Klings in southern Thuringia. (Photo: Thüringisches Landesamt fur Archäologische Denkmalpfelge)

were interpreted as the result of a mass slaughter that followed the defeat of the settlement in a conflict. However, it seems that no evidence for weapons injuries has been established for any of the 'victims' and it seems that the mass burials are more likely to be the remnants of a votive ritual practice. However, there is some evidence for an attack on the site – damaged arrowheads made of bronze and also of stone and bone were found by a ditch while a single male skeleton discovered in a trench above the ditch was lying next to a bronze arrowhead that could have been the cause of his death. This settlement has not been fully excavated and the possibility remains that our understanding of the nature of these burials may be improved by further work (Tihelka 1969).

One final example is that of a young female body from Stillfried in Austria. This girl (12 or 13 years old) was found under the late Urnfield Period rampart of the site and appeared to have suffered savage wounds. Her skull shows four large circular perforations and a

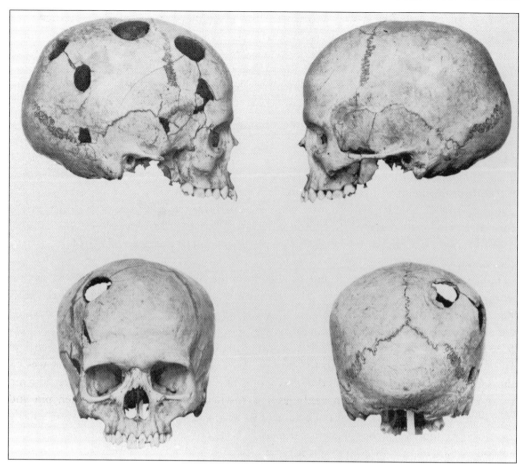

Fig. 4.4. The girl's skull from Stillfried in Austria, displaying severe trauma. The circular perforations through the skull may have been the result of human sacrifice, or the final blows of an attack. (Photo: by courtesy of Prof. Dr C. Eibner and Dr M. Teschler)

couple of smaller puncture wounds (**Fig. 4.4**). It has been suggested that the initial blow, from an attacker on her right, was dealt to the right brow resulting in a large puncture wound and probably her death. After this, other blows rained down on her now prostrate body. The interpretation of the pattern of wounds suggests that the temple was pierced by the blade of a sword while the later, circular, wounds were caused by the pommel of this weapon. Perhaps a more plausible explanation for these circular wounds might be that they were dealt by some sort of club or mace, if they were from an attack (Breitinger 1976).

WEAPONRY

Many of the weapons and forms of armour familiar throughout Bronze Age Europe originated, at least in terms of design, in central Europe. This region was vital to the whole network of Bronze Age trade, with metalwork, often weapons, being exchanged for amber, furs and textiles from the north and west, and for goods such as oils and wines from the south. The fact that weaponry of a central European origin appears in southern Europe in the Bronze Age is beyond dispute and, although mercenaries may have been responsible for the presence of some weapons, trade with the region is the most obvious explanation. Although there must have been a strong prestige and display element to weaponry, most of it was functional and could certainly have played a deadly role in Bronze Age combat. Fortunately much Bronze Age metalwork survives in central and eastern Europe.

As in northern and western Europe the bow and arrow was a major weapon at the start of the Bronze Age in central and eastern Europe, and was used both for hunting and for combat. The archaeological record retains the material traces of such weaponry in the form of arrowheads made of flint, bronze and even bone. At its clearest level, in terms of proof of use in fighting, arrowheads are found embedded in victims. Carvings also portray these weapons.

Flint arrowheads have been found on sites from the Neolithic and Copper Ages, such as Brailiţa and Varna in the Balkans. The tradition of flint arrowheads in archery certainly persisted into the Early Bronze Age Únětice Culture period of Central Europe. At Adlerberg in Germany tanged flint arrowheads were found in graves. Flint arrowheads have also been recovered from a series of graves around Celle (near Hannover) in Germany, at Bleckmar and Baven for example (Coles & Harding 1979: 297). As well as the arrowheads, bronze spears and daggers, pins and ornaments were also recovered from these graves. Grave 1 at Baven held eleven arrowheads together with a rapier, pin and dagger. Bows and arrows were important in other parts of the study region in the Early Bronze Age, such as in the Oberpfalz region of Germany and in the Únětice Culture sites of south Thuringia where arrowheads have been found buried with warriors. Bronze arrowheads and a sword were recovered from a Middle Tumulus Culture grave at Hloubětín in the Czech Republic. Although perhaps superseded by the spear as the main projectile weapon by the Urnfield Period, it is probable that archery remained important throughout the Bronze Age both for hunting animals and for killing humans.

The earliest bladed weapon in the region was the dagger, the forerunner of the rapier and the sword. This would obviously have required warriors to engage in very close combat, as opposed to the bow and arrow. Daggers are not only found in graves – their presence in the hoards of the Early Bronze Age is also well documented. Such votive hoards played an important part in the Únětice Culture where objects such as daggers and halberds are often found with an innovative handle form: a solid metal hilt cast on to the object. An example of such a hoard from Bresinchen and Dieskau (von Brunn 1959: plates 12–23) in central Germany contained halberd blades, flat axes, amber beads and arm rings among other bronzes. Another came from Łęki Małe in Poland. Halberds were thought to have been used as a pole-arm, with the dagger-like blade attached at a right angle to the end of the shaft and used in a sweeping motion. Such a weapon would have been tricky to use in combat and thus perhaps they were geared towards more display-orientated functions.

The dagger, a stabbing bladed weapon, was followed by the dirk and rapier in the Middle Bronze Age. These later stabbing weapons were themselves replaced by the more versatile sword, a weapon that could be used in a stabbing or slashing action. The sword probably developed in central Europe towards the end of the Middle Bronze Age and could take many forms, both in terms of blade and also of handle. Initially the swords were like rapiers in that they were long and thin, with relatively weak rivet attachments at the top of the hilt. Soon, however, the handles became solid (the so-called Vollgriffschwerter) or at least had proper hilts with wooden or bone plates (Griffzungenschwerter). By the end of the Bronze Age these hilts were increasingly ornate. The antennae-hilted swords had tightly spiralled projections at the end of the handle, which are reminiscent of an insect's antenna. With the change in handles came a similar change in blade shape, from the long thin early forms to the leaf-shaped later types more suited to the classic 'cut-and-thrust'-style weapon. Many swords throughout the region display damage and nicks to the blade which may perhaps indicate that they were used in fighting. However, it was not unknown for these swords to be deliberately bent or broken to 'destroy' them; for example, a bent sword found at Rydeč in Bohemia had been ritually killed in this way. Perhaps, like King Arthur's Excalibur, they were destroyed on the death of the warrior to placate the deities, or such finds might represent the destruction of an enemy's weaponry, the reuse of which might have been taboo.

Throughout the Bronze Age the sword continued in importance across central and eastern Europe, both as weapon and prestige object, and has only relatively recently relinquished this position – in the last hundred years or so. Their ritual importance can be seen in a couple of hoards at Hajdúsámson in Hungary and Apa in Romania. At both sites the swords were laid out alongside a series of battle-axes. The former site was especially spectacular as the leaf-shaped sword with a solid bronze hilt and rich decoration had no fewer than twelve bronze battle-axes, many of which were also highly decorated, laid across it (Sherratt 1987: 54).

Axes themselves can be interpreted as weapons, and they are found in our period with the copper flat axes and the stone battle-axes of the Corded Ware groups of central Europe. But it is my belief that axes, along with palstaves, were not used in combat during the Bronze Age, especially when so many alternatives were available. Axes were objects of great beauty and could have been prestigious objects in their own right, performing a ceremonial role. In addition they did have a functional purpose once hafted, but this was probably more for cutting wood than for fighting.

The spear, by contrast, was of great use in combat. Early variants of spear-style weapons were more knife-like in form, with a blade and a tang to fit into the shaft. The classic socketed spearhead emerged at the end of the Early Bronze Age and examples are found throughout central and eastern Europe, in hoards, graves or as isolated discoveries. Perhaps this weapon, although usable as a projectile, was more suited to a thrusting action at arm's length. The evidence of a spear retained in the body at Hernádkak in Hungary is perhaps indicative of this.

At the climax of the Bronze Age swords and spears would have been the vital weapons of the warrior. That is not to say that bows and arrows and daggers were not used at all, however. Perhaps even axes were used at times. Certainly arrows are still found in Late Bronze Age funerary contexts.

DEFENSIVE EQUIPMENT

Shields

Some of the finest examples of European Bronze Age armour are found in the panoply of defensive objects from the region. The warrior in central and eastern Europe could call upon shields, helmets, breastplates and greaves for protection (or for use in ceremonies). The sight of a warrior fully caparisoned in bronze armour and holding a gleaming sword would have been very impressive. It seems likely that shields would have been made from either leather or wood for actual combat. In terms of finds of such shields, we have examples from Wollmesheim and Mehrstetten in Germany (Coles 1962: 172). Thanks to poor pre-excavation survival conditions these shields are now only evident through the metal studs they originally featured. The Wollmesheim shield, the 'type-find' for this group, still retained fragments of the wood around the studs, enough to indicate that the original thickness of the shield was around 2cm. This shield was found in association with a leaf-shaped sword and socketed arrowheads. It has been suggested that the Mehrstetten shield, found in the 1905 excavation of a barrow, was around 80cm in diameter – some 30cm larger than the wooden example from Annandale described in Chapter Two. Both shields have been dated to the start of the Urnfield Period.

Several 'U-notch' shields (so-called after the U-shaped notch within the circular strengthening ribs present on the face of these shields) have been recovered from central Europe. Two were found in Ostprignitz, Germany, and were of fairly similar design to the Danish shield from Taarup Mose. The Pilsen-Jíkalka shield from Bohemia is another member of the U-notch group, though in this case the notch is more crescent-shaped. Found in 1869 around 0.5m away from the site of a hoard found a week previously, the shield has been assigned an early Urnfield date (Coles 1962: 162).

A further group of shields belong to the Nipperwiese class. These possess two annular strengthening ribs, without a notch, and have a handle riveted at the back. Nipperwiese shields have been found at Spalt in Bavaria and at Mainz and Bingen in Germany, alongside the type-site of Nipperwiese itself (now called Ognics) in Poland (Coles 1962: 162).

The Bingen shield, found in the River Rhine, is particularly interesting (**Fig. 4.5**). A round shield of 393mm average diameter, it had lost one section of its rim which had broken away along a fracture and displayed other damage, including a tiny elliptical perforation that could have resulted from the thrust of a weapon tip (Needham 1979: 115). If so, it is perhaps of similar value to the Nipperwiese shield from Long Wittenham for indicating the use of these cast shields in combat alongside the probably more frequent use of sturdy organic-material variants.

Corselets and greaves

In addition to shields from the early Urnfield Period, we also find protective body armour. Beneath the huge burial mound at Čaka in Slovakia were a number of graves, one of which contained many fragments of a sheet bronze corselet with decorative bosses and rivets. At an average of 1mm thick, it would perhaps not have been of great functional

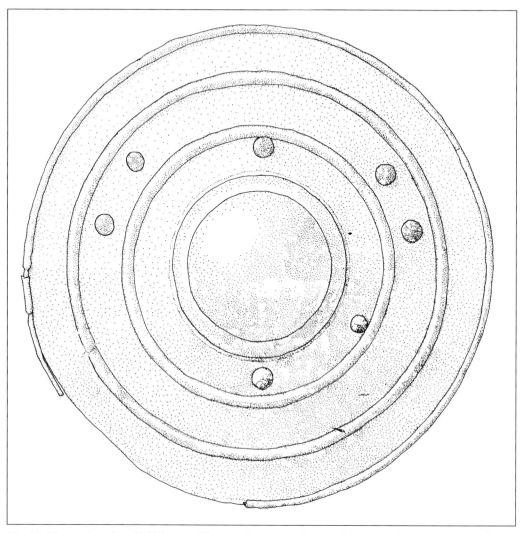

Fig. 4.5. Nipperwiese-class shield from the Rhine at Bingen, showing possible weapon damage. (After Needham 1979)

value but may reflect the fact that body protection was now deemed important, and thus indicates that examples of a more sturdy, utilitarian material such as leather were possibly in use (Točík & Paulík 1960) (**Fig. 4.6**).

A series of Urnfield Period greaves have been uncovered in the southern part of the study region (**Fig. 4.7**). At the site of Rinyaszentkirály near Somogy in Hungary we have an example of greaves that had been decorated with water-birds – a recurring theme of the later Bronze Age, perhaps connected to the importance of water in the votive practices of the age (von Merhart 1958). Beneath a Late Bronze Age burial mound at Ilijak in Bosnia were a series of greaves bearing ornate decoration, including a depiction of a deer on one example.

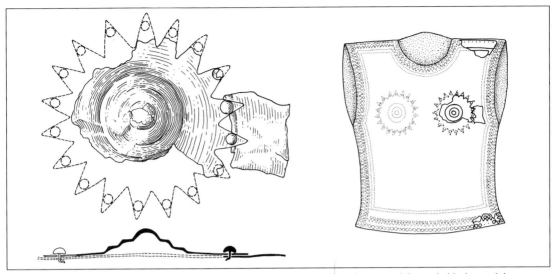

Fig. 4.6. The Caka corselet: (a) surviving fragments; (b) a reconstruction drawing of the probable form of the original. (After Točík & Paulík 1960)

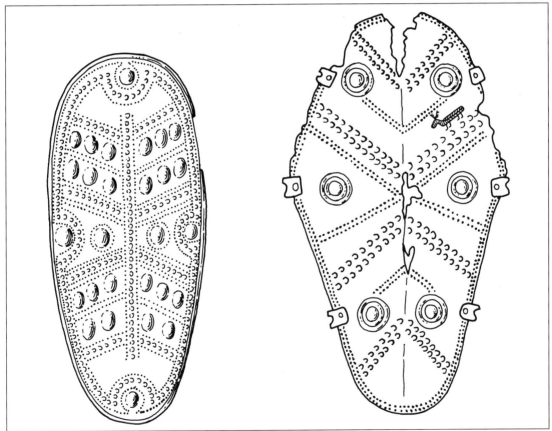

Fig. 4.7. Bronze greaves: (a) Kurim; (b) Ilijak. Greaves protected the warrior's lower legs and were probably for ceremonial use. (After von Merhart 1958)

Fig. 4.8. The Pass Leug helmet, Austria. This object has an ornate crest and hinged cheek-pieces, which have circular beaten designs on them. (Photo: Carolino Augusteum – Salzburger Museum für Kunst und Kulturgeschichte)

Helmets

A number of helmets, often quite elaborate and varied in form, have been discovered throughout central and eastern Europe. As with much of the protective panoply, these generally date to the Urnfield Period, reflecting increasingly skilled metalworking techniques throughout the region. These helmets range in type from conical-bell finds at Lúčky and Spišská Belá in Slovakia, Beitzsch and Oranienburg in Germany and Keresztéte in Hungary, to the crested and round types. An elaborate example of the crested helmet group was found as part of a small hoard at Pass Lueg near Salzburg in Austria. This helmet, basically a conical cap, not only had a crest; it also had a pair of cheek-pieces attached by wire (**Fig. 4.8**). Crested helmets without such cheek-pieces but still impressive have been found at numerous other locations such as Kleinhüningen, Baden, Lesum, and

Pockinger Heide in Germany. A further example is the important Urnfield hoard from Hajduböszörmény in northern Hungary which included the helmet, highly decorated solid-hilted swords, a bronze axe, a bronze *situla* (bucket) and a bronze cauldron with bird protomes (Hencken 1971).

In summary, the full range of Bronze Age defensive accoutrements was available to combatants in the Urnfield Period of central and eastern Europe. Although many of these exquisite bronzes may well have been used in displays of a ceremonial nature, they are indicative of a heightened technological skill but also probably reflect the presence of sturdy organic, protective variants. Certainly such parallel examples exist within shield technologies and perhaps are depicted by some dramatic rock carvings.

ICONOGRAPHY

Although the region under discussion does not have the elaborate rock-carvings of Scandinavia, Italy or Spain, we none the less do have interesting iconographic information from central and eastern Europe. Of particular importance to this study are the carvings from Petit Chasseur, in the Rhône Valley in Switzerland (Gallay 1978). Although Copper Age in date, these well depict the warrior at the start of the Bronze Age (**Fig. 4.9**). These anthropomorphic figures were found in chamber tombs, as are representations of bows and arrows, and show a possible quilted costume on the human figures. Perhaps these are warriors clad in quilted armour armed with bows and arrows. Quilted armour is particularly effective against archery and there are numerous examples of it in the ethnographic record; perhaps its last appearance in action was at the battle of Omdurman in Sudan. Again these carvings point to the fact that organic examples of armour were functional and they may well have continued in use throughout the Bronze Age, as did shields of organic material, while metal examples like that from Čaka, were primarily for display purposes.

In addition to these figures from Switzerland, we find numerous anthropomorphic statues from the other side of our study area, in eastern Europe. One example from Natalivka near Dnepropetrovsk, Ukraine, is of a male figure holding what looks like a bow in its left hand and in its right a shafted hand-axe and a mace or some type of club. Another, from Hamangia near Dobruja in Romania has axes depicted on its back and male genitalia on the front, and perhaps even the hint of a corselet (**Fig. 4.10**). These are both Early Bronze Age examples from the Catacomb Period. A third statue depicts a human figure upon which two smaller figures, perhaps fighting, are shown (Gimbutas 1965: 496). A large standing stone from Tübingen-Weilheim, Baden-Württemberg, Germany, is inscribed with five halberds carved in relief on to the sandstone alongside a possible bow.

The bow is thus depicted in early iconography in this area just as it was in the examples of Scandinavia in Chapter Two. The axe is represented as well. The later period is less rich in artistic depictions of warriors – we do find images of figures with spears on the 'face-urns' of the Baltic countries but these are from the later Hallstatt or Early Iron Age periods. In addition, the famous Late Bronze Age Strettweg chariot (**Fig. 4.11**) has a number of figures, several of which are mounted warriors with shields, spears and crested

Fig. 4.9. One of the anthropomorphic stelae from Petit Chasseur in Switzerland. A depiction of a bow is clearly visible. (Photo: H. Preisig, Musée Cantonal d'archéologie, Sion)

helmets, probably very similar to examples dated to the end of the Bronze Age in central Europe. A couple of the warriors hold what look like hafted axes.

A possible portrayal of a warrior in ceremonial action is found on a decorated urn of the Middle Bronze Age (around 1300 BC) from Vel'ke Raškovce, Trebišov in Slovakia (Pare 1999: 126). This urn, from a cremation grave of the Suciu de Sus culture, bore incised decoration depicting several wagons, each being pulled by two horses, behind which stood a human figure perhaps with sword and even helmet. Wagons of the period were sturdy, bulky affairs – hardly the sort one would associate with chariot warfare, but suitable for ceremonial activity. That we might see a warrior following such a vehicle perhaps indicates the cult importance of martiality in the period.

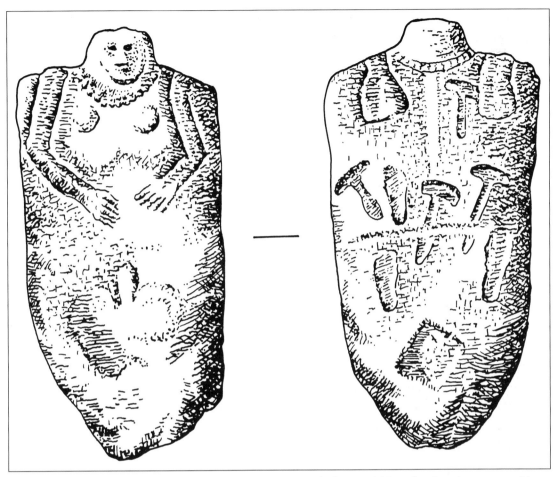

Fig. 4.10. Anthropomorphic stela from Hamangia in Romania. The figure is 1.95m tall and carries weaponry; his genitalia and a possible corselet are also depicted. (After Gimbutas 1965)

CONCLUSIONS

Many of the innovations and vital elements of the Bronze Age originated in central and eastern Europe. Settlements in the region were ideally located to benefit from trade with both the north and the south. Goods such as amber, furs and textiles from the north were exchanged for oils and wine from the south. Settlements grew up along rivers and land passes but were subject to raids and thus required the building of defences, particularly from the Urnfield Period onwards. Many other elements of Bronze Age society hint at the occurrence of conflict, the scale of which will always be difficult to gauge.

At the start of the Bronze Age in the region, the bow was the dominant weapon, just as it was in northern and western Europe. It seems likely that the warrior was provided with some sort of protective clothing: padded armour is effective against arrows and may even be depicted in the rock carvings of Petit Chasseur in Switzerland. The lethal effects of

Fig. 4.11. A mounted warrior from the Strettweg chariot, armed with a spear and protected by a shield and helmet. This cult chariot is thought to be Late Bronze Age in date. (Photo: Landesmuseum Joanneum, Bild- und Tonarchiv, Graz)

archery are revealed by the remains of those probably killed by arrowheads from sites like Klings and Stetten in Germany. Early Bronze Age warriors were also equipped with daggers and perhaps halberds and axes, though doubts remain over the functional viability of the latter two as weapons types.

The portrayal of people as warriors (or at least as owners of prestige weaponry) was vital to Early Bronze Age cultures. The Helmsdorf and Leubingen burial mounds of Germany are especially spectacular examples of this, but similar burial rites were found on a smaller scale throughout much of the region. Although it is usually assumed that burials with weapons are those of males, more palaeopathological work needs to be undertaken

Fig. 4.12. The Bronze Age warrior. (Kenton White)

on the skeletons before such sweeping generalisations can be confirmed. Recent excavations at Pokrovka in Russia have revealed burials of females with weaponry including bronze arrowheads and iron swords. Women could certainly have fulfilled the role of combatant in Bronze Age warfare.

As the Bronze Age progressed, warriors were able to use spears, rapiers and, ultimately, leaf-shaped swords. Metalworkers produced exquisite bronze helmets, corselets and greaves, too. These objects are generally the ceremonial equivalents of functional variants constructed from sturdy organic materials such as leather and wood. In the Urnfield Period bronze horse harness – such as the bridle and stirrup bars from Crailsheim and Wallerfangen in Germany – became increasingly common, perhaps illustrating the heightened importance of the horse. Horses would have been very significant for warriors, giving extra mobility over land just as boats were vital for passage along rivers. The use of the horse spread from this region to western Europe, though we should not think in terms of modern cavalry.

Champions performed the major roles in fighting of the Tumulus (and related) Cultures of central and eastern Europe, with combat perhaps of a more 'showy' and ritualised nature than later in the Bronze Age. This being said, raiding and attacks by war-bands would also have been a threat. With boats and horses assisting with mobility, raiding was almost certainly the prevalent form of conflict in the Late Bronze Age, not only for prestige trade goods but also for land as pressure increased. Raids on the settlements along the trade-routes resulted in the great fortified sites of the Urnfield Period. It is unlikely that such settlements escaped attack in the Early Bronze Age. The stakes were very high, for the victor would gain land, prestige goods and perhaps even slaves through fighting, while the vanquished were taken as slaves if they survived the fighting. Certainly combat in the region had a propensity to be both brutal and deadly.

FURTHER READING

Bóna, I. 1975. 'Die Mittlere Bronzezeit Ungarns und ihre südöstlichen beziehungen', *Archaeologia Hungarica* 49

Carman, J. & Harding, A.F. 1999. *Ancient Warfare* (Sutton)

Coles, J.M. 1962. 'European Bronze Age Shields', *Proceedings of the Prehistoric Society* 28: 156–90

Coles, J.M. & Harding, A.F. 1979. *The Bronze Age in Europe* (Methuen)

Harding, A.F. 2000. *European Societies in the Bronze Age* (Cambridge University Press)

Härke, H. 1979. *Settlement Types and Settlement patterns in the West Hallstatt Province: an Evaluation from Excavated Sites Europe* (British Archaeological Reports International Series 57)

Hencken, H. 1971. *The Earliest European Helmets: Bronze Age and Early Iron Age* (Peabody Museum, Harvard University)

Patay, P. 1968. 'Urnenfelderzeitliche Bronzeschilde im Karpatenbecken', *Germania* 46: 241–8

FIVE

ITALY

INTRODUCTION

Bronze Age Italy has left a rich archaeological legacy, including abundant evidence for the importance of warfare. As with Europe north of the Alps, Spain and Greece, there is a treasure trove of bronze weapons and a variety of defended sites, while the idea of the warrior is represented by weapons and armour in burials as well as by armed figures depicted in rock art, on statue stelae and in bronze.

The geography of Italy has left an indelible mark on its cultural history. What we now call Italy consists of two large islands (Sicily and Sardinia), several groups of tiny islands and a long, narrow peninsula projecting southwards from mainland Europe over 1,000km into the Mediterranean, and divided by the great spine of the Apennines which cuts off the centre from the north, and the east from the west. In addition, climate, access to natural resources and proximity to lands beyond Italy vary across the peninsula and islands. This geographical diversity is mirrored in the cultural make-up of Italy, then as now. It is characterised by shifting patterns of regional differences in industrial activity, burial customs and material culture. For, while the physical configuration and distribution of natural resources stay the same, relationships between different groups, and levels of prosperity change. So, for example, Sardinia and Tuscany have rich metallurgical deposits which aided their prosperity and at times attracted foreign interest, while Sicily has less metal but could profit from trade in native amber, alum, pumice and rock-salt, and benefited from its position in the Mediterranean as an obvious stopping-off place for sea-borne traders heading east or west.

Various types of warfare must have taken place in Bronze Age Italy, from larger battle campaigns to minor local disputes. It is possible that small-scale raiding to capture livestock, foodstuffs and women was common both on land and at sea. The long coastline of Italy and her position in the middle of the Mediterranean make seafaring a certainty from earliest times. Both archaeological evidence and documentary sources show that sea travel and sea trade were integral to the functioning of many Mediterranean communities. The corollary to regular, large-scale sea trade is conflict on the high seas, from piracy to major sea battles. A Mycenaean fresco shows a sea battle, but the evidence from Italy comes from later periods. Sea battles were occasionally depicted on pottery, for example the Aristonothos crater from Cerveteri, dated *c.* 650 BC, shows a confrontation between (?)Etruscan and Greek ships, both bristling with armed warriors. There are also passages by Greek and Latin writers lamenting piracy, remarking on Etruscan control of the Tyrrhenian sea, and recording sea battles in Italian waters involving Greeks, Etruscans and Phoenicians.

Fig. 5.1. Map of Italy, showing places mentioned in the text.

One of the common reasons for warfare has always been the desire to take control of natural resources, trade-routes and other sources of wealth. The archaeological evidence suggests that trade and the accumulation of wealth were important elements in the story of warfare in Bronze Age Italy, as elsewhere in Europe. Sicily and southern Italy provided ports of call for various Bronze Age groups trading in the Mediterranean. From Greece came the Mycenaeans in the Middle Bronze Age, attested by Mycenaean pottery at many southern sites. Contact with Greece ceased after the collapse of the palatial civilisations, but was renewed in the Early Iron Age when Greek traders and colonists came flooding west: the earliest known Iron Age western Greek settlement was sited on the tiny island of Ischia in the bay of Naples in the eighth century BC, and many more followed in the south and on Sicily. Trading contacts with the Near East, especially Cyprus and the Levant, continued through the Middle Bronze Age into the Early Iron Age almost uninterrupted, though at varying intensities. The Phoenicians traded with and settled in Sardinia from the end of the Bronze Age and not long after established colonies and trading sites in western Sicily and elsewhere in the central and west Mediterranean. Sicily had particularly wide-ranging contacts: hoards and tombs of Middle Bronze Age date and later contain material from peninsular Italy, Sardinia, southern France, Iberia and northern Europe, as well as from the east Mediterranean. The development of fortified coastal sites from the Early Bronze Age in Sicily and neighbouring islands must owe something to this pattern of trade, as must the rise of a rich Bronze Age culture on Sardinia and the elaboration at native sites of impressive defences, especially when Phoenicians settled on the island from the ninth century BC.

Similarly, control of land routes into Europe north of the Alps benefited various groups in northern Italy, especially those in the hills above Liguria in the west and Venice in the east. It is no surprise that we find defended upland sites in these areas developing in part as a response to regular trading across the Alps and the local desire to control and profit from that trade.

People travelling for trade pass on ideas as well as raw materials and finished objects. In the context of warfare there was the transfer of technological innovations, such as the introduction and development of certain forms of sword and spearhead to Italy from Europe north of the Alps.

CHRONOLOGICAL NOTE

The Copper Age in Italy dates from *c.* 3000 BC onwards, and the Bronze Age roughly from the end of the third to the beginning of the first millennium BC. Recent dendrochronological and radiocarbon dates have pushed the beginning of the Bronze Age in northern Italy back from the eighteenth to the twenty-first century BC. The evidence includes oak posts found at the palafitte sites of Lavagnone and Barche di Solferino in the Lake Garda and Val d'Adige areas (Cocchi Genick 1996). At the other end of the period, recent work on the dendrochronology of the Swiss sites, combined with shared bronze types north and south of the Alps, suggests that the Italian Early Iron Age began at the latest in the tenth century BC. This chapter includes events in Italy down to the later eighth century BC (into the Early Iron Age) to allow comparison with events in Late Bronze Age Europe north of the Alps.

SETTLEMENTS AND FORTIFICATIONS

Italy has some outstanding defended sites. The most striking, abundant and best studied are the *castellieri* of northern Italy and the Sardinian stone-towers known as *nuraghi*. These may be seen in the context of a general trend in Europe in the rise, development and use of fortifications.

The settlement evidence for Italy is very diverse, with many regional variations, and differing preservation and levels of research. For some areas and periods very little is known, for example the Copper Age in most regions is principally known from the burial record. There are few studies of single regions and settlement types, defining their formal characteristics and date ranges of occupation, to compare, for example, with the detailed work on central European hillforts. This section focuses on the sites with impressive defences and good defensive potential.

It is interesting that there is a tendency for settlements to be placed where they may take advantage of natural defensive potential: on hilltops, promontories, and so on (Peroni 1994), suggesting that the possibility of self-protection was often a factor in the choice of site location, even if the defensive potential was not always exploited. For example, there are many Bronze Age upland/hilltop sites in the Apennines which have great defensive potential. But on the basis of climate, geographical location and archaeological deposits (including the size of the site), many of these sites have been interpreted as shepherds' camps occupied only in the summer when flocks were taken to the high pastures. Location alone is generally insufficient evidence for warfare, and we need additional evidence such as man-made fortifications.

The elevated fortified sites known as *castellieri* in the east and *castellari* in the west are found in the Alpine arc of north Italy. Some three hundred are known in the Maritime Alps, distributed from Liguria to southern France, while there are at least seven hundred in north-east Italy, and many more further east in Croatia and Slovenia (where they are known as *gradine*). *Castellieri* have substantial walls of rough-hewn limestone blocks and rubble. Some have multiple walls with terraces between them on which were built stone huts. The north-western sites have received less study but seem to have first appeared in the third millennium BC, with most probably dating to the first millennium.

Those in north-east Italy have been better studied (for example Karouškova-Soper 1983), though the number of excavations remains low, and precise dating is difficult in many cases. They are mainly located in the Karst – upland limestone – landscape, where there are poor water resources and thin soils. The altitude of these sites is usually around 200m, but can rise to over 2,000m. They lie on natural ridges and plateaux often only 1–2km apart. Many are only around 50m in diameter, though some are much larger. The dry-stone walls could originally have reached a height of 4.5m, and formed a single enclosure, or one main wall with smaller internal enclosures which might have been used for livestock. The entrances can be simple or reinforced with semi-circular bastions.

The earliest examples date to the eighteenth century BC and some were in use into the Roman period. Lack of excavation and the nature of the evidence from such sites means that date ranges are available for only a limited number, but some *castellieri*, such as Elleri, Storje and Monrupino, were apparently occupied uninterrupted for almost a thousand years.

Some *castellieri* were too inaccessible to have functioned as permanent settlements and could have served as look-out posts, summer camps for shepherds, sanctuaries or small farmsteads: there are occasional traces of wooden huts and burials. Others are large well-fortified sites in key positions near main trade-routes.

The area lacks natural resources (apart from stone) and the geology and climate are such that the dominant mode of subsistence at these sites was probably pastoralism. The *castellieri* may reflect the need to defend the livestock from raiding neighbours, and also competition for pasture, water and access to the sea (Karouškova-Soper 1983). Some might also have developed in response to trade. Central European hillforts group around major trade-routes, and seem to flourish and decline with the use of each route, thus implying a close relationship between trade and the need to defend the control of that trade and the profits gained from it. Many *castellieri* tend to cluster around the major routes into Italy from north of the Alps and from the east, and are thus strategically placed to benefit from control of these routes. It is likely that the main routes across the Alps, and some subsidiary ones, were all in use through the Bronze Age, but the relative importance of each differed. The east and west routes into Italy may well have shifted in popularity during the Bronze Age and Early Iron Age (Sherratt 1993), with a Danubian route – reaching Italy from the north-east via the head of the Adriatic – being most popular in the Copper to Early Bronze Age and in the Later Bronze Age, and an Alpine route from the north-west and swinging down into Liguria – dominant in the Middle Bronze Age and Early Iron Age. The Danubian route underlay the prosperity of the Early Bronze Age Unětice and Otomani cultures of central Europe, and the Alpine route that of the Middle Bronze Age Tumulus Cultures of northern central Europe (*see* Chapter Four). Bronzes from all these cultures reached Italy.

Mediterranean sea-borne trade may be important in the development of some fortified sites in the south, a region which has links with the east Mediterranean through much of the prehistoric period. For example, proto-urban centres developed in the south, especially in Sicily, in the Middle Bronze Age, profiting from sea trade especially with the Mycenaean world. A number of these proto-urban centres were fortified.

As early as the Copper Age, some settlements in Sicily were surrounded by stone enclosure walls or ditches, and by the Early Bronze Age there were stone-built enclosures and turreted walls at coastal sites, which became important as regional centres and trading stations in the Middle Bronze Age (Leighton 1999). They include the major trading site of Thapsos in south-east Sicily which is located on a promontory above a good harbour. The promontory is connected to the mainland by a narrow isthmus and the natural defences were enhanced in the Early Bronze Age with a substantial curved fortification wall nearly 200m long with six semi-circular bastions, protecting a settlement area in which there are signs of urban planning by the Late Bronze Age. Other sites with simple massive enclosure walls include Torricella overlooking the plain of Catania. Similar enclosure walls also occur in Bronze Age Apulia at some coastal sites, and elsewhere in the Mediterranean, including some of the small islands close to Sicily. The site of Mursia on Pantelleria lies on a natural platform overlooking the sea, and is further protected in the Early Bronze Age by a wall 200m long and 7m high. By the Middle Bronze Age Ustica, a small island off north-west Sicily, could boast the coastal settlement of I Faraglioni with a massive perimeter wall and ten projecting semi-circular towers (**Fig. 5.2**). Some inland sites are also impressive,

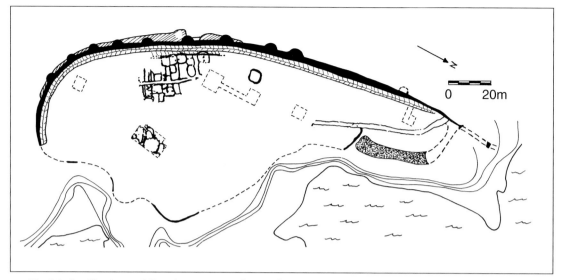

Fig. 5.2. Fortifications at I Faraglioni, Ustica (after Leighton 1999, fig. 82).

for example Pantalica, located in a river valley inland from Syracuse in south-east Sicily. This site includes an acropolis protected by walls, one with a trapezoidal tower.

The Sardinian *nuraghi* form a distinctive class of fortified site. Over seven thousand are known, of which most take the classic form of a single conical tower built of large, shaped stone blocks. The walls are up to 4m thick, and the towers have one entrance, interior chambers on one or two storeys with domed or corbel-vaulted ceilings, and often stairways built into the walls. The dating of the *nuraghi* has been problematic but as more excavations are carried out and better dating evidence is recovered, especially radiocarbon-datable material, a picture is emerging of classic *nuraghi* having developed by 1500 BC (i.e. early in the Middle Bronze Age) and possibly a few centuries earlier.

The classic *nuraghi* seem to have developed out of 'corridor' or proto-*nuraghi* which are square or round in plan and contain only narrow passages or corridors. Given their form, and the fact that they are low, and generally not visible from afar, it has been suggested that they were actually raised platforms for huts (themselves not stone-built) with the internal passages used for storage (Trump 1992). Thus they need not be interpreted as primarily defensive in function. However, the classic *nuraghi* are obviously effective as fortifications with their high, robust walls and single entrance. This impression is further enhanced by some cast-bronze models of *nuraghi* which have walls enhanced with battlements and machicolations. It is not clear exactly how these *nuraghi* were used or what they symbolised. Many scholars think they were the fortified residences of warring local elites. Certainly they would have been effective against raiding parties: their height makes them effective look-out stations and there is enough space inside to hold a small community, although hardly enough to house more than a few dozen animals as well. They should probably also be seen in terms of claims to land, perhaps status, and possibly also as statements of power – none of which need conflict with their defensive potential.

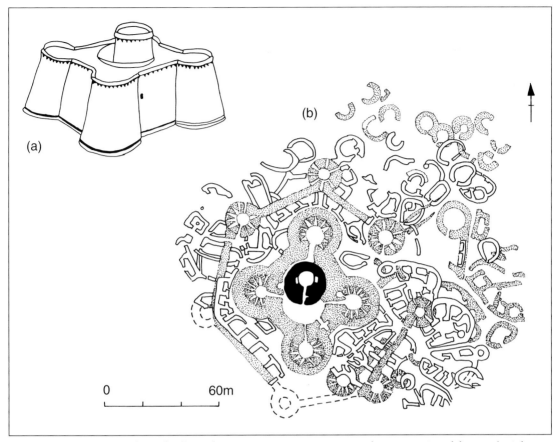

Fig. 5.3. Complex nuraghe *with village of Su Nuraxi, Barumini. (a) proposed reconstruction of the* nuraghe *(after Peroni 1994, fig. 10.3); (b) plan with three phases, black is the earliest phase, the classic* nuraghe; *stippled is the second phase, the complex* nuraghe *and part of the village (after Piggott 1965, fig. 89).*

It is striking that some areas have great concentrations of *nuraghi*: for example in part of east central Sardinia, twenty-nine *nuraghi* are clustered in an area of just 40 square kilometres.

The later Bronze Age saw the development of multiple or complex *nuraghi*, and towards the Early Iron Age nuragic villages began to appear. The impressive, fortress-like complex *nuraghi* have a central tower surrounded with additional towers or bastions, linked by wings often with internal corridors. The complex of towers may also be enclosed within a robust stone circuit wall. Good examples are those of Su Nuraxi at Barumini (**Fig. 5.3**) and Sarròch at Antigori, the former with four large bastions around the central tower and a circuit wall with smaller bastions.

Nuragic villages consist of clusters of stone-built houses and other small structures around classic or complex *nuraghi*, and generally date from the Early Iron Age onwards. Excavations have been carried out at two modest inland nuragic villages in Nuoro province (Michaels & Webster 1987). They lie 1.5km apart and each had a heavy stone circuit wall. One (Toscano village) covered an area of around 10,000 square metres. The central tower produced very little domestic debris of the Iron Age, and the excavators have suggested that the tower was not used primarily as a residence.

Nuragic sites, especially the complex *nuraghi* and nuragic villages, reflect the increasing wealth and complexity of Sardinian society in the Bronze Age and Early Iron Age: there are rich deposits of metalwork, and evidence not only for metal-working and long-distance trade in bronzes and other items but also for elaborate cult observance. Pottery and other goods from the east Mediterranean also reach nuragic sites, even ones far inland, especially from the Middle Bronze Age onwards. For example, at the site of Sarròch there was a large room containing local pottery and hundreds of Mycenaean vases, plain or painted, of later Mycenaean date (*c.* 1340–1110 BC) from Cyprus, Crete, Rhodes and maybe Argos on mainland Greece. Peaceful cohabitation between locals and presumably Mycenaeans – and perhaps other East Mediterranean people – is indicated by this abundance of pottery and also by non-Sardinian cult observance inside the *nuraghi*. Mycenaean pottery also occurs elsewhere, as do bronzes with Mycenaean and sub-Mycenaean influence (and imitations of them), Cretan-type swords and Baltic amber. Although the palace economies of Greece collapsed trade continued in the Mediterranean and Sardinia flourished.

WEAPONS AND ARMOUR

Bronze weapons form an important category of archaeological evidence for the Italian Bronze Age. Technological improvements occur throughout the period, presumably prompted by the practical need for better weapons. For example, blades were attached more firmly to hilts using tangs and sockets, and became more robust and better shaped for stabbing and withdrawing from wounds. Weapons come principally from burials, hoards and ritual deposits in watery places and on hilltops. Armour is much rarer and is generally found in burials of the later Bronze Age and Early Iron Age. While most phases saw 10 per cent or less of all bronzes (including weapons) being deposited ritually in water or on hilltops in the peninsula and Sardinia, this rose to a striking 65 per cent (Peroni 1994) in the Middle and early Late Bronze Age, when there was a corresponding reduction in deposition in burials and non-votive hoards.

Hoarding began early, almost as soon as the potential of metal as a means of accumulating more wealth was realised and there was enough metal around to provide a surplus, and became increasingly common from the Early Bronze Age onwards. Hoard is a blanket term covering a wide range of deposits varying in size, content and archaeological context. Many hoards consist of a small number of items probably forming ritual deposits and these vary in quantity over time. Some hoards may have been collected together with exchange or trade in mind, such as the group of twenty-five fine, unused, solid-hilted triangular daggers of Bohemian type from the Ripatransone hoard, Ascoli Piceno (**Fig. 5.5d**), or hoards containing Italian-made axes; most of these, not surprisingly, are located near the major metal deposits of northern Tuscany. Others may be a collection of worn, broken, unfinished or miscast items and ingots, the objects having been gathered together to be recycled locally or perhaps exchanged in wider trade networks. An example is the Late Bronze Age hoard from Lipari, weighing 75kg and stored in a jar below a floor.

In the Copper Age burials provide the best evidence for weapons, with barbed and tanged flint arrowheads being common, together with daggers made of flint and copper. The introduction of bronze brought innovations in weapon and tool forms: the flat axe became flanged, the shaft-hole axe was developed and the solid-hilted dagger appeared (some with finely engraved decoration on the blade and hilt) along with the halberd. Many of these bronzes show close links with examples from Austria, Germany and Bohemia, for example the daggers in the Ripatransone and other hoards. Such daggers also occur as single finds as far south as Matera. The later Cascina Ranza hoard (Milan) contains south German swords, socketed spearheads and Swiss-type flanged axes.

The Middle Bronze Age saw the disappearance of flint daggers and stone battle-axes, and the increasing rarity of flint arrowheads. Daggers were common, but the great innovation was the long sword. Concentrations of sword types, which paralleled or were related to types from north of the Alps, occurred in the Alpine arc – exactly where one would expect them to be. Elements of horse harness in antler and bone are found for the first time in Italy.

The later Bronze Age is divided into the Recent and Final periods. The Recent period saw some continuity of weapons types from the Middle Bronze Age with swords and daggers as the most distinctive weapons, found in tombs and hoards. The socketed spearhead became common from the Final Bronze Age onwards, and this period was also marked by a qualitative and quantitative leap in the production of bronze artefacts, matching a similar process across most of continental Europe. Daggers were still used, but primarily in Sicily and Sardinia.

In the Early Iron Age there was generally a great increase in the numbers of weapons placed in tombs, though there are regional differences, with weapons – many in iron – initially being more common in burials in the south (for example at the Calabrian site of Torre Galli) but later the phenomenon spread northwards. In the later ninth century, and especially in the eighth, there were a number of rich burials with panoplies including a sword, one or more spearheads, an axe and one or more pieces of parade armour in the form of embossed sheet bronze helmets, shields and pectorals. Such burials are very similar to the Urnfield warrior phenomenon north of the Alps. Pottery skeuomorphs of bronze helmets are also found.

As in many other areas of Europe, it is likely that the bow and arrow was one of the main weapons used in fighting in the Neolithic and Copper Age in Italy. Copper Age burials frequently contain barbed and tanged flint arrowheads (as many as forty in a tomb). The remarkably well-preserved equipment carried by Ötzi the Iceman included a quiver of arrows and a long bow, both in need of repair or completion (Spindler 1994). The quiver of goat skin over a hazelwood frame was broken into three pieces, and the 6ft long bow of yew wood was unfinished – the ends not yet grooved to hold the bowstring. There were fourteen arrow shafts (thirteen of viburnum and one of dogwood), only two of which were fitted with flint arrowheads and threefold feather fletching at the base. The careful choice of appropriate woods, together with the

Fig. 5.4. Sardinian archer figurine. (Reproduced by courtesy of the British Museum)

fourteen other types of wood represented in his equipment, reminds us how much information is generally lost to the archaeologist by the normal processes of decay and decomposition of organic materials, and how skilled the prehistoric makers were in choosing the right materials for the task.

In addition to practical needs, some Neolithic and Copper Age arrowheads were very beautifully made with long delicate tangs – the shape and quality dictated more by aesthetics than practical requirements. These beautifully made prestige stone weapons went out of fashion with the coming of bronze. There is little archaeological evidence in Italy for the use of the bow and arrow after the Copper Age and Early Bronze Age: there are no depictions in rock art or on statue stele, and relatively few arrowheads are found in any context. There are some bronze examples, either socketed or tanged, both types with a triangular blade and wings at the base. The striking exception is the large number of nuragic warrior figurines equipped with a bow (*see* pp. 107–8). These bows come in two forms: curved and reflexed, possibly long and composite. Presumably the bow and arrow was still in use in the later Bronze Age and Early Iron Age, especially for hunting (for which it is one of the most practical weapons), but for various reasons it was not considered appropriate for inclusion in burials and hoards, or in most iconographic representations of hunting and warfare.

Daggers (defined here as two-edged blades generally under 30cm in length) are the earliest blade weapons in Italy, as elsewhere in Europe. Like swords, they can have solid cast, composite or organic hilts, the latter two being partly or wholly of bone, antler, ivory or wood. Those with solid cast hilts are rare and confined to a small group of types from the earlier Bronze Age and have close links across the Alps. There are just over 1,700 daggers recorded for peninsular Italy alone dating to the Copper Age and Early Iron Age (Bianco Peroni 1994). They are particularly abundant in the earlier periods, when they occur in a wide range of types and probably served as both weapons and knives. Daggers are important both functionally and symbolically in the Copper Age and earlier Bronze Age, as shown by their relatively abundant deposition in tombs and hoards, and depictions on statue stele and in rock art. Two-thirds of the daggers found in peninsular Italy date to the Middle and Late Bronze Age, which is surprising given that the sword was introduced at the beginning of the Middle Bronze Age and the knife proper (single-edged blades) in the Late Bronze Age. Both the sword and the knife replace functions of the dagger, but it obviously remained socially valued and significant for some time. Fewer than twenty of the daggers found in peninsular Italy date to the Final Bronze Age or Early Iron Age, and they are essentially foreign to the peninsula, having come from, or been inspired by, Sardinia and Sicily where the dagger was still a popular and important weapon. A small number of Sardinian examples turn up across the Tyrrhenian sea in Early Iron Age Tuscany, and a few Sicilian-style daggers have been found in Calabria.

The halberd was a curious and somewhat unsatisfactory weapon made briefly in the Copper Age and Early Bronze Age in response to the need to put a dagger on a long shaft. The blade resembled contemporary daggers (**Fig. 5.5c**) and was attached at right angles to a long shaft, and used in a sweeping motion. It was awkward to use, and probably not very robust, the blade easily breaking loose from its rivets. It was later replaced by the far more efficient and versatile spear and sword. Only a few dozen halberds are known from Italy (Bianco Peroni 1994), and some are depicted in rock art, but there are none on statue stele or held by nuragic figurines.

Nearly four hundred swords have been recorded from peninsular Italy alone; they date from the Middle Bronze Age to the Early Iron Age (Bianco Peroni 1970). Italian sword use often paralleled that of central Europe, with the introduction of the rapier and its replacement by the slashing sword, but as always in Italy there were regional patterns with, for example, the dagger remaining popular alongside the sword especially in the south and Sardinia. The types show diverse sources of influence and origin, as would be expected given Italy's location. A series of swords closely related to types north of the Alps (and even to some examples imported from central and eastern Europe) is concentrated in the Alpine arc in the Middle Bronze Age, indicating the intensity of traffic over the Alps. These include the Sauerbrunn type (**Fig. 5.5e**), whose distribution in Treviso and other parts of the Veneto (the far north-east of Italy) may be related to the amber route through central Europe from the Baltic, reaching Italy on the Adriatic side. Four examples of the Rixheim type (and a number of very similar swords) have been found in the Recent Bronze Age in tombs near rivers and terramare

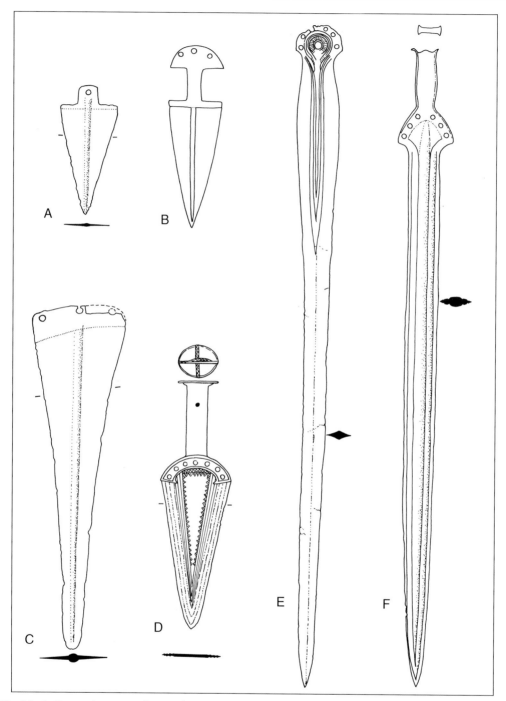

Fig. 5.5. A: Copper Age copper dagger of Remedello type (after Bianco Peroni 1994: 1); B: Remedello-type dagger carved on stele Bagnare A (after Anati 1972, fig. 70); C: Halberd from northern Italy (after Bianco Peroni 1994: 35); D: Central European-style dagger, Ripatransone hoard (after Bianco Peroni 1994: 408); E: Middle Bronze Age, Sauerbrunn-type rapier, northern Italy (after Bianco Peroni 1970: 1); F: Late Bronze Age tanged slashing sword, Treviso (after Bianco Peroni 1970: 126). A–D and E–F are drawn at different scales.

Fig. 5.6. Part of Area 1 of the Great Naquane rock, Valcamonica (after Anati 1961: 34–5).

settlements in Lombardy and Emilia-Romagna, thus lying at the edge of the type's principal distribution in central Europe. Some western European/Atlantic sword types reach Italy, especially Sardinia. There are also some east Mediterranean sword types coming into the south and Sardinia, for example the Surbo hoard (Lecce) includes a Mycenaean sword fragment.

Spears were common from the Late Bronze Age onwards, and occur in many burials and hoards on mainland Italy and Sicily. They are useful when thrown from long distance, and when used as a thrusting weapon in close combat. The long shaft could also be used as a 'war-stick'. Various authors have used length to distinguish between spears (for thrusting) and javelins (for throwing), but the distinction may not be this simple, and smaller spears could obviously be used in both ways. Spearheads are often accompanied by a ferrule, also socketed, and most are pointed as if for sticking the shaft into the ground. Spearheads often occur in 'warrior' burials alongside other weapons in the later Bronze Age and Early Iron Age (**Figs 5.8, 5.9c**) especially in peninsular Italy. They are one of the weapons most often brandished by figures in Valcamonican rock art where they are used to spear both animals and humans (**Figs 5.6, 5.12**), but only one nuragic figurine carries a spear, suggesting that this weapon was not popular in Sardinia at this time (or perhaps was not thought generally appropriate in this iconographic context).

The axe was multi-purpose and came before the sword as a hafted middle-distance weapon. The axe was often associated with other weapons in tombs (*see* **Fig. 5.8e**) or on statue stele (*see* **Figs 5.9, 5.10**), and it may be that after going out of fashion as a practical weapon it was retained for symbolic purposes. As noted elsewhere, axes occur in various Early Iron Age tombs, including some rich female tombs of the eighth century which contain no other weapons or armour.

The knife could also be used in many different cultural contexts, from the kitchen to the sacrificial altar, as well as in hunting and warfare. Knives only come into the archaeological record in the Recent Bronze Age, and prior to that it is likely that the wide range of daggers acted as both weapons and knives.

Finally there is the vague category that includes the club, 'war-stick', etc. Many of the Sardinian statuettes carry what have been interpreted as 'war-sticks' (Stary 1991), and some figures in rock art seem to be carrying clubs or sticks. Actual examples have not yet been recovered (or perhaps have not been recognised) archaeologically.

DEFENSIVE EQUIPMENT

Defensive arms and armour consisted of items to protect the body: helmets, chest, arm and leg protection, and shields. These must have been used throughout the period and most were probably made of toughened leather and other organic materials, but few actual examples have survived. In contrast, we do have the elaborate, embossed sheet bronze items which must have been used for parade and ceremonial purposes, being too elaborate, unwieldy and fragile for use in battle.

It is likely that helmets were in use throughout the Bronze Age, and most were probably made in leather for practical purposes. There are hints of their use in the iconography,

Fig. 5.7. A selection of protective clothing and helmets worn by Sardinian figurines (after Stary 1991, figs 1–2, 4–12, 15).

with some hunter/warrior figures in the northern rock art wearing what seem to be elaborate spiked or plumed headdresses or helmets (**Fig. 5.6**). A great variety of helmet forms are worn by the nuragic warrior figurines, including some with long curving horns, others with a strange single projection rising from the front and folding over (the so-called caterpillar form), and those with a crest of feathers (**Fig. 5.7**). There is no way of telling whether these represent different types of real helmet, and whether they were all in use at the same time. Early Iron Age sheet bronze helmets from central Italy adorn select rich male tombs as part of an Urnfield-style warrior panoply (Hencken 1971). The helmets are crested (**Fig. 5.8**) or knobbed, with embossed decoration which may include the bird in sun-boat motif also found across central and northern Europe. In the proto-Etruscan area in the Early Iron Age these helmets are copied in pottery and used to cover some cinerary urns. They are interpreted as indicating a male burial of a particular rank or status. Eighth-century burials from Verucchio have preserved organic materials including a woven wicker cap helmet with attached iron discs and central spike.

Chest protection comes in various forms, hardened leather probably being the most common material. The beaten sheet bronze cuirasse, often with rich embossed decoration, occurs from quite early in the Urnfield Period in central Europe. That none has been found in Italy dating to the Bronze Age or Early Iron Age is probably an accident of discovery/preservation. Otherwise there are small chest protectors in sheet bronze – pectoral plaques which protect only the central part of the thorax.

The Sardinian warrior figurines wear various forms of leg protection, from simple knee-guards to guard-plates and greaves, as well as a kind of boot or legging (**Fig. 5.4**). Greaves are rarely preserved but occur from the Late Bronze Age onwards, for example the pair from Torre Galli, Calabria, dating to the Early Iron Age. The common form is an oval bronze sheet, richly decorated, and with rings along the edge, to which were attached the ties.

Shields must also have been in common use, mainly made in hardened leather, no examples of which have been found. A number of warriors in rock art appear to be carrying small round shields, and many of the nuragic figurines carry small round shields with central bosses and the outer surface divided into wedges which are covered with parallel lines. The Early Iron Age sees the deposition in some wealthy male 'warrior' tombs of large, finely made and decorated embossed sheet bronze shields (**Fig. 5.8**). These continue into the Orientalising period in rich 'princely' tombs, and one example was ritually deposited in a sanctuary at Tarquinia (Bonghi Jovino 1986: 100–5), together with a decorated bronze axe and a *lituus* (a long ceremonial bronze horn). These shields seem to be much larger than those held by the nuragic figurines, making them rather unwieldy. Their size together with the fragility of the bronze and the elaborate decoration all point to their use as prestige parade items.

The use of the horse seems to have spread across the region from the Middle Bronze Age, with, for example, antler cheek-pieces being found at settlement sites in the north. Horse harness in bronze and/or iron becomes relatively common in the Early Iron Age, and there is also increasing evidence for the use of chariots and carts – starting with fragments of iron wheel bands in a couple of eighth-century tombs, and by the later eighth and seventh centuries BC there are a number of wealthy tombs containing whole chariots, and occasionally also horses. Interestingly, some seem to belong to women, and as these tombs have no weapons or armour presumably the chariot here is an indication of high status rather than of participation in warfare. It is hard to gauge the extent of use of horse and chariot in Bronze Age warfare in Italy. Presumably the primary use for chariots was in parade and other ceremonial occasions.

The use of miniature or skeuomorph weapons and armour through the period reinforces the symbolic significance and social importance of the warrior and warfare. The Copper Age sees the production of flint copies of copper daggers, sometimes even copying the rivets on the hilt, and miniature weapons in bone or stone occasionally occur from this period onwards. For example, bone daggers and axes were found at the palafitte site of Barche di Solferino (2150–1980 BC) in the northern lakes area, and at Tanaccia di Brisighella. Stone axe pendants are also known, for example from the Copper Age Cellino San Marco rock-cut tombs in south-east Apulia. Some miniature daggers come from Middle Bronze Age tombs in the south at sites such as Pantalica and Dessueri.

Miniature weapons and armour (swords, daggers, spears, shields, pectorals) also occur in central Italy in the Early Iron Age, for example in a few tombs in the Latial cemetery of Osteria dell'Osa, often in association with the rare hut urns (miniature pottery skeuomorphs of huts). It is likely that these objects mark out leading male members of the community (Bietti Sestieri 1993). In contemporary cemeteries north of the Tiber there are full-size pottery skeuomorphs of bronze helmets, both knobbed and crested, which are used as cinerary urn covers, and again mark particular male roles or status.

BURIALS AND PALAEOPATHOLOGY

Italian prehistory is rich in burial evidence – indeed for some periods and regions this is almost the only type of evidence recovered. As contexts which represent deliberate, highly structured ritual observance, burials potentially offer information about beliefs and social structures. From the Copper Age onwards there are phases in which weapons are deposited as grave-goods – a varying proportion of those given formal burial are represented as 'warriors' in burial.

The use of rock-cut tombs with collective burial is a more Mediterranean than central European feature in the Bronze Age. It began in the Copper Age and in some places continued through the Bronze Age, for example in parts of Sicily. Otherwise, single burials occur in the Copper Age period and became increasingly common in small groups; by the Early Iron Age there are cemeteries which may contain thousands of individual burials.

Copper Age tombs are relatively abundant and are important contexts for metalwork, including weapons and armour, as are Late Bronze Age to Iron Age tombs. A good example from the Copper Age is the cemetery of Remedello, near Brescia, dating to around 2500 BC. It has 117 inhumation burials, some containing copper flat axes, triangular daggers, halberds, and barbed and tanged flint arrowheads. There are also flint daggers imitating the copper ones and flint winged arrowheads. The latest tombs at the site are associated with Bell-beakers, copper daggers and wrist-guards. The Rinaldone Culture of Tuscany, Umbria and Latium also produced some tombs with these 'warrior' grave-goods. Barbed and tanged arrowheads are common, and are deposited in various quantities up to about thirty.

Relatively few Early and Middle Bronze Age tombs have been found and not many contain metal goods. The majority of bronzes are deposited in hoards which continue to be important into the Early Iron Age. In the Late Bronze Age archaeologically visible burials became more abundant, especially with the introduction of small cremation cemeteries of central European Urnfield type. The grave-goods are generally poor but include some weapons.

Cemetery size increased throughout the Bronze Age and by the Early Iron Age there are some in central and northern Italy containing thousands of burials. Complex gender and other social distinctions were made in burials, with small numbers of men being buried with one or more pieces of weaponry and armour and varying combinations of other artefacts – pottery, personal ornaments, utensils and bronze vessels. The proportion of such burials varied across Italy, but the highest numbers were concentrated in western Italy from Calabria to Tuscany. It may be no coincidence that it was in this area (excluding Calabria) that Etruscan and Latin city-states soon developed. A prime example is the eighth-century tomb (AA1) from the cemetery of Quattro Fontanili at Veii just north of Rome (**Fig. 5.8**). This cremation burial contained various pots, personal ornaments and an impressive panoply including a sheet bronze parade shield and crested helmet, a bronze axe and spearhead with ferrule, a short sword with iron blade and bone and ivory hilt, and a sheet bronze scabbard. In addition there were two iron horse-bits with bronze cheek-pieces (suggesting the use of a chariot) and a sheet bronze urn for the ashes. All the sheet bronzes were richly decorated, the motifs including the solar bird-boat of central Europe origin. This seems to be an Italian version of the Late Bronze Age Urnfield warrior tombs found north of the Alps. The rarity of the bow and arrow in these later Bronze Age and Early Iron Age burials may be because it was not a weapon used in heroic face-to-face combat, and thus did not fit the image of the Urnfield-style warrior any more than it suited the Homeric warrior of Bronze and Iron Age Greece.

For some people at least, burial as a warrior must have been symbolic of social status rather than evidence that the deceased had served primarily as a warrior in life. For example, the Quattro Fontanili cemetery contained the inhumation burial of a child around six years old whose rich grave-goods included a full-size sword and spear.

As noted elsewhere in this book, even with good skeletal data it is not possible to assess accurately the number of individuals who suffered fatal or non-fatal injuries as a result of warfare. Many injuries, even fatal ones, may be flesh-wounds leaving no mark on the skeleton; spear and dagger thrusts to the vital organs, and sword cuts to main arteries, can all kill quickly, while minor flesh wounds may fester and cause death from gangrene. Apart from the frozen body of Ötzi, the Iceman, which retains skin and flesh, bodies survive only as skeletal remains varying in degree of preservation and completeness. Bone preserves well in certain soils, for example those in the Remedello cemetery in northern Italy, while in areas of acid soil, such as the volcanic zones of west central Italy, all that remains are often fragments of long bones and dental enamel. Cremation was used extensively in the Late Bronze Age and into the Iron Age and these remains may be incompletely gathered from the funeral pyre, and in any case are very broken and distorted making the work of the bone analyst even harder. An additional problem is the uneven and relatively low frequency of bone analysis.

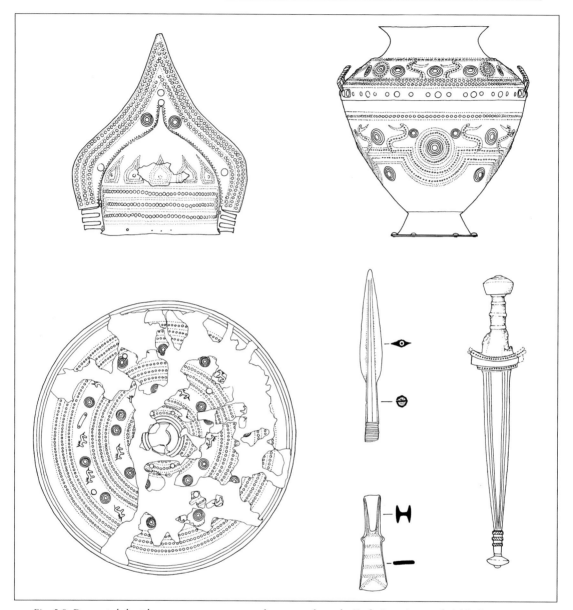

Fig. 5.8. Decorated sheet bronze armour, an urn and weapons from the Early Iron Age tomb AA1, Quattro Fontanili, Veii (after Notizie degli scavi 1971, *figs 72, 74, 77, 82).*

Interpretation of injuries often depends on the context. For example, a Rinaldone Copper Age tomb from Ponte San Pietro, Tuscany, contained two bodies: a male 'warrior' accompanied by pottery, a stone axe, fifteen barbed and tanged arrowheads, two copper triangular daggers, and an awl; and a female with pottery and a bead necklace. The female had a skull injury. This type of trauma could easily be the result of warfare, but given the circumstances of her burial some scholars have speculated that the woman was ritually killed to accompany the male warrior to the grave.

In one sample of almost a thousand individuals from the Bronze Age only ten skeletal traumas were found (Robb 1997a). Given the incomplete nature of many of the skeletons examined, and the fact that this is not a representative sample from all phases and all parts of Italy, we cannot tell what the total skeletal trauma rates were in Bronze Age Italy, but they can hardly have been high. How many of these might have been the result of warfare? It is hard to tell in most cases, but some were examples of trepanning and it is safe to assume these were not warfare-related.

A few suggestive cases have been published, such as a Beaker period burial from Marcita-Castelvetrano, Sicily, which has a healed dent at the front of the skull, and a Copper Age skeleton from Elba with a lesion apparently caused by a blow or blows from a polished stone axe.

The present evidence from Italian skeletons is thus rather limited. There are few examples of skeletal trauma which might be the result of warfare, and there are no unusual accumulations of bodies outside normal cemetery areas, of the type found in Spain (*see* pp. 45–8).

ICONOGRAPHY

Italy has produced splendid iconographic evidence for the importance of the warrior in Bronze Age society. There is a rich and varied iconographic tradition with rock carvings, statue-stelae and bronze figurines as the major categories, all incorporating images of weapons and armed figures.

Sardinian bronze figurines form a striking body of evidence (**Figs 5.4, 5.7**). Around five hundred are known, of which over eighty are warriors or related figures sporting a great variety of weapons and armour. Most scholars date the statuettes to around the eleventh to seventh centuries BC. The statuettes come from nuragic contexts, with over thirty found at one site (Teti, prov. Nuoro). They are individually modelled and cast in the lost-wax method, and are distinctive in style, with long wedge-shaped faces, large eyes, hands and feet, and clothing and equipment rendered in detail. Most wore protective clothing, probably of leather, often doublets which may have added shoulder protection, while some wear long skirts with bosses, possibly representing bronze discs. Armour also includes pectorals, spiral neck-guards, and various forms of leg protection from simple knee-guards to greaves. All but one wear helmets, half of which are horned, and many carry a round shield with central boss. The main weapons are the war-stick, bow and arrows, dagger and sword. There seem to be different sets of equipment (Stary 1991). For example, a quarter of the statuettes are equipped with a combination of helmet, doublet, round shield and war-stick and often also greaves and a dagger. An even more popular combination, sported by almost half the figures, is a helmet (generally horned), doublet and bow, and most also have a pectoral, sword or dagger, and greaves (**Fig. 5.4**). Interestingly, the bow is not found in combination with a shield, even though many of the archers carry a sword or dagger.

The weapons and armour of the figurines are so varied and specific that it is tempting to think that they were drawn directly from life. If so, do they represent the full range of

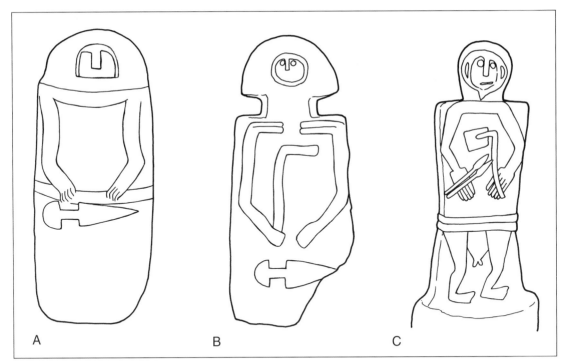

Fig. 5.9. Three styles of statue-stele from the Lunigiana. A: Pontevecchio; B: Filetto or Malgrate; C: Reusa (after Anati 1981, figs 27–9.)

actual warrior types, a select group of them, or even a series of ceremonial outfits? If these statuettes are any indication of the range of battle panoplies actually in use in Sardinia at the time, then it seems that many warriors used the bow and arrow at a distance, and the dagger or sword for close combat, while others were equipped only for close combat, lacking the bow and arrows and instead having a war-stick and dagger or sword and added protection from a shield. Strabo (V.2.7) described Sardinian armour in the late first century BC as including mouflon hides, light small leather shields, short daggers and swords, which echoes some of the statuettes. Curiously, only one carries a spear, although this is a common weapon in the later Bronze Age and Iron Age archaeological record for Italy, including Sardinia. Also odd is the fact that the popularity of the bow here is not paralleled in other Italian archaeological contexts. These apparent contradictions are hard to interpret. Do they indicate that Late Bronze and Early Iron Age Sardinian warriors were unusual in using the bow, or does it mean that only a selection of the full range of weapons was deposited in burials and hoards, and depicted in rock art and on statue-stele? The war-sticks carried by so many statuettes may have been commonly used elsewhere in Italy, but do not survive because they were made of wood.

It is not known who had access to the figurines, whether it was the whole community or a restricted sector of it. In contrast, the two other main sources of iconographic evidence for warfare (rock art and statue-stelae) must by virtue of their location have been visible to anyone passing by over long periods of time. Statue-stelae have been found in various parts of northern Italy, with the largest number (over fifty) coming from the Lunigiana region south-east of Genoa (**Fig. 5.9**). There are around fifty more elsewhere: smaller groups in the Alto Adige, Valcamonica, Valtellina and Val d'Aosta, some stelae in and around Bologna, and a few isolated examples in Val Germanasca in Piedmont and Triora in western Liguria. The stelae are monolithic, carved, incised and may be coloured. Colour was found on a few examples such as one from St Martin de Corléans, Aosta, and colouring materials were found in Valcamonica. Most of the stelae have highly stylised anthropomorphic forms, and some bodily features may be explicitly carved. The date range seems to run from the end of the Neolithic to the Iron Age, with a large number in the earlier Bronze Age if the weapon forms are any indication of date. They form part of a more widespread Bronze Age tradition: statue-stelae also occur in south-west Switzerland at Sion, in southern France as far west as the Aveyron area, in Corsica and parts of Spain. And even further away, there are stelae in Germany, Romania, the Ukraine and the Crimea.

The Lunigiana stelae are the most explicitly anthropomorphic of the Italian examples (**Fig. 5.9**). They were set up on the hills between the Magra river and the Alpi Apuane, up to a height of 700m. Some were found in groups, for example a line of nine found at Pontevecchio. They vary in height from about 0.5 to 2.5m. Over fifty stelae have been found so far, of which twenty-seven are complete, or almost complete. Of those which are sufficiently complete for all features to be seen, nineteen have been identified as male by the presence of weapons. The stelae are divided into an upper portion which forms the head, and a lower, larger zone for the body. The arms are simply carved, generally bent at the elbows, and weapons may be held in the chest area, or sit below. The stelae become more naturalistic over time: the earliest 'Pontevecchio' group is the most stylised with simple face and no neck, the 'Filetto or Malgrate' group have a distinct but still very stylised head, while the 'Reusa' group have more facial features and sometimes legs carved in relief. The commonest weapons on the stelae are daggers, generally lying horizontally below the arms. One late example has a dagger with antenna hilt apparently suspended from a belt on the side of the stele. Some figures carry an axe, of which there are two forms, identified by scholars as of Bronze Age and Iron Age dates. A few figures also carry a pair of pointed objects, which are probably spears scaled down to fit on to the stelae. One curiosity is that the stylised heads of the Filetto/Malgrate group are exactly the same shape as the pommel of the daggers on the same stelae (**Fig. 5.9b**), implying that the stelae themselves may represent both bodies and weapons.

How can these stelae be read? Do those with weapons represent warriors? If so, does that mean that axes were used in battle? Or were axes symbols representing some position of power, like the later Roman *fasces* (axe and bundle of rods) carried by lictors to proclaim the powers of a magistrate to punish and execute? It is interesting to note in this context that some wealthy female tombs of the eighth century BC from Etruria contained one or two axes, together with elaborate jewellery, spinning equipment, pottery and other grave-goods. It is most unlikely that these axes indicated warrior status as the tombs contain no other weapons or armour.

A smaller group of statue-stelae from the Alto Adige is rather different in form and decoration. They are roughly shaped rectangular blocks with what might be a fringed belt carved across the middle. Some stele carry images of weapons. It might be a single dagger

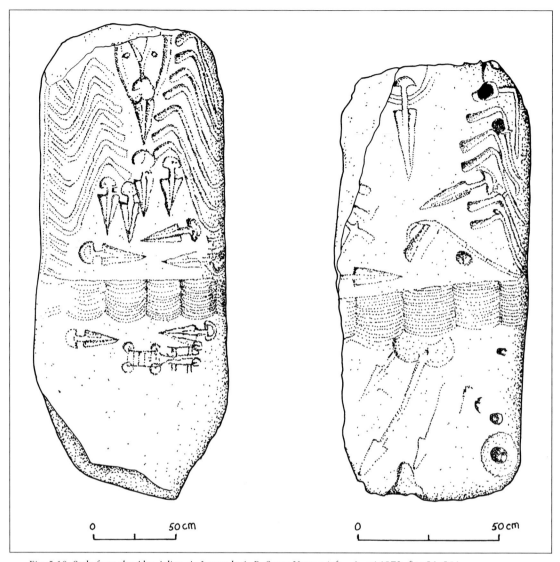

Fig. 5.10. Stele from the Alto Adige. A: Lagundo 1; B: Santa Verena (after Anati 1972, figs 54, 56.)

lying horizontally above the belt, or multiple daggers and other weapons variously arranged over the body of the stelae. Lagundo 1 and the stele from Santa Verena (**Fig. 5.10**) are striking examples of the latter. Lagundo 1 has two daggers below the belt together with a four-wheeled wagon drawn by two bulls, and above the belt are eight daggers, one of which seems to form part of a stylised face, and resembling multiple arms there are seven hafted axes on each side above the belt. The Santa Verena stele also has multiple axes and daggers, and emerging from below the belt are a pair of discs and a spear(?), suggestive of male genitals. Again we see a mixing of images with weapons doubling up as body parts.

Rock art occurs in the north Italian Alps, down into the coastal region west of Genoa and across the border into France, with major concentrations in the Valcamonica (about 90 per cent) and on Monte Bego (about 90 per cent of the rest). Thousands of individual carvings have been recorded, from small groups to large collections across an outcrop like the Naquane rock at Valcamonica which has nearly nine hundred carvings in nine groups. Some collections seem to have been built up over time and it is often difficult to tell how the separate elements are meant to relate to each other, if at all. Rock carvings are hard to date: apart from some objects which seem sufficiently similar to actual objects (such as halberds and Remedello daggers), there is little or nothing in the images themselves to provide dating and no reliable scientific methods have been developed for dating the incisions in the rocks. However, most scholars accept that the carvings probably range from the later Neolithic to the Iron Age. As in rock art in other parts of Europe the subjects include figures, weapons and other implements, animals, buildings and various symbols. The scales of people, animals and objects are not in proportion – a dagger can be the same size as a deer.

Weapons, by themselves or wielded by humans, are common. One rock, known as the Caven 2 stele, Valtellina (**Fig. 5.11**), has one human holding aloft a halberd(?), and other weapons scattered around: Remedello-style daggers and three hafted axes. The carvings on the Naquane rock include 172 figures, some armed with spears, dagger/sword, round shields, elaborately plumed headdresses or helmets and a few halberds, axes and sticks. A common combination is a spear and shield, both held aloft. Some are hunting deer with spears, on foot or horse, and a small number are in combat. Yet others brandish weapons but are isolated, or at least far enough from their enemy or prey that we cannot identify them. Deer hunting is clearly an important element in the imagery; stags are identified by large Christmas tree-like antlers (*see* **Figs 5.6, 5.12**).

While there are some images of warriors in conflict, these are very much in the minority, and the overall reading of such rock faces is by no means clear. The presence of animals, often deer, implies that hunting is as important an activity as warfare in these images. Hunting and warfare both require similar qualities: bravery, intelligence, determination, physical strength and dexterity, skill in the use of weapons, a respect for and understanding of the prey or opponent, and a willingness to take life. Are we seeing in the rock art the confluence of the two activities as a package of male roles both carrying a rich freight of symbolic values for these prehistoric communities? This confluence certainly seems present on a small number of bronze sword scabbards from Early Iron Age tombs which carry incised images of huntable animals (mainly deer) and sometimes a hunting scene. The scabbards form part of warrior burials, and are obviously prestigious, prized pieces of equipment, primarily indicating a warrior ideology, with a clear but subordinate reference to hunting.

CONCLUSIONS

The archaeological evidence suggests that warfare was a significant feature of Italian Bronze Age life, and the warrior a key image for the age. The abundance of weapons, the series of fortified sites and the rich iconographic tradition show that warfare not only took

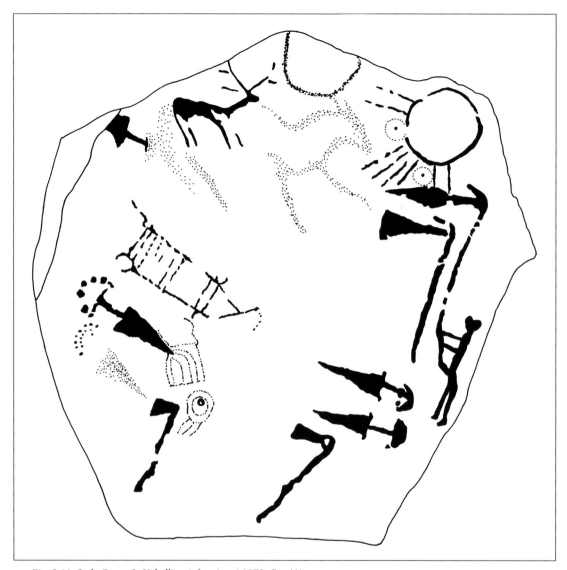

Fig. 5.11. Stele Caven 2, Valtellina (after Anati 1972, fig. 41).

place but was also important in the ways Italian Bronze Age societies represented themselves in burial, ritual deposits and public images.

In antiquity, as in many later pre-industrial societies, aggressive impulses were often channelled into hunting and warfare – providing food, exercise and training in various skills, and protecting the community against external threats. In addition, the exercising of these skills could be important in rituals, such as puberty rites, and social structures within which rank and prestige could be conferred on the basis of excellence. A corollary is the use of the warrior (and hunter) as primary images for

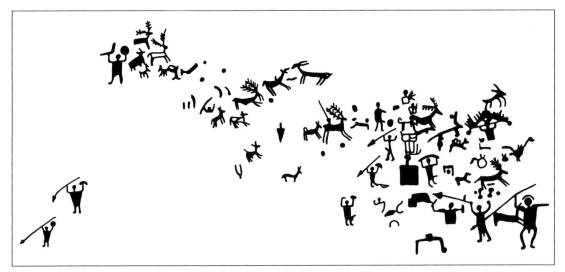

Fig. 5.12. Part of Area 5 of the Great Naquane rock, Valcamonica (after Anati 1961: 44–5).

society – displayed on ceremonial occasions, and in art and literature (as in the Homeric epics).

Conflict can involve varying degrees of organisation and numbers of participants, from small-scale opportunistic raiding (on land and sea), to ritualised raiding parties, organised competitions, seasonal brief battles with neighbours and longer war campaigns. We can speculate about the causes of warfare – presumably they were varied and often complex – but it is likely that the desire to acquire or protect sources of wealth often played a role. It is surely no coincidence that many of the fortified sites are well located for trade, or are near metal and other valuable deposits. There is a fine line between trade and warfare, and that line must often have been crossed.

The possession of elaborate defences and weaponry does not necessarily mean that fighting was a common event. On the contrary, they indicate to others that you are prosperous, prepared to engage in war and feel confident of success, and thus they may have a powerful deterrent effect. In addition, impressive defences, statue-stelae and large rock faces covered with engraved images are visibly and permanently part of the landscape and may be used to bolster the power of certain groups in the society, to recall the ancestors and so on.

To what extent did the Italian Bronze Age male define himself in terms of a warrior identity? How often does one have to take up arms to feel one is a 'warrior', or that the concept of a warrior, living in a society in which there have been and are still great warriors, is important? It is conceivable that many in Bronze Age Italy led relatively peaceful, rural lives, travelling little, engaging only in local conflicts, and taking part infrequently in larger-scale organised warfare. However, they might have sat by the fire at night and heard tales of great warriors and famous conflicts. Men could be defined by their role as warriors, whether or not they actively took part in warfare, ever or occasionally, to the point where in the Early Iron Age a person was given a warrior role in burial even though he was unlikely to have undertaken the role in life (a boy under ten years old was buried with full-size weapons). Here the weapons must have had primarily a symbolic value.

The warrior was often represented as the single champion or hero in hand-to-hand combat with dagger or sword and spear, and maybe also armour. The fabulously arrayed Urnfield warrior is the elite Bronze Age warrior at his most impressive. This was presumably not the norm for the battlefield, the sea battle or the cattle raid, in which leather armour and a wider range of weaponry, including the bow and arrow, would have been used. Just as today's greyhound-thin models, icons of the present age, stand out as unusual in daily life, so the Urnfield warrior, clothed in elaborately decorated sheet bronze armour and wielding fine, expensive weapons, was no doubt not representative of the average person's experience of war in the Bronze Age. Societies have often created images of heroes and heroines embodying desired qualities and identified by distinctive physical characteristics, clothing and equipment. It has been argued that in Bronze Age Italy, as elsewhere in Europe, burial and iconography were used, in part, to express publicly ideals of masculinity and femininity (for example Robb 1994; 1997b). The preferred image of femininity seems to have been one of personal adornment – prominent females are often buried with elaborate sets of jewellery – as well as domestic virtues which are embodied in the spinning and weaving equipment so common in burials, and masculinity was represented by the cult of the hero, displaying prowess as warrior and hunter.

FURTHER READING

Coles, J.M. & Harding, A.F. 1979. *The Bronze Age in Europe* (Methuen)

Harding, A. 1994. 'Reformation in barbarian Europe, 1300–600 BC', in B.W. Cunliffe (ed.), *The Oxford Illustrated Prehistory of Europe* (Oxford University Press), pp. 304–35

Leighton, R. 1999. *Sicily before History* (Duckworth)

Robb, J. 1997b. 'Female beauty and male violence in early Italian society', in A.O. Koloski-Ostrovo & C.L. Lyons (eds), *Naked truths: women, sexuality and gender in classical art and archaeology* (Routledge)

Santillo Frizell, B. (ed.). 1991. *Arte militare e architettura nuragica (Nuragic architecture in its military, territorial and socio-economic context)*, Conference proceedings: Skrifter utvigna av Svenska Institutet i Rom, 4°, xlviii

Sherratt, A.G. 1994. 'The emergence of élites: earlier Bronze Age Europe, 2500–1300 BC', in B.W. Cunliffe (ed.), *The Oxford Illustrated Prehistory of Europe* (Oxford University Press), pp. 244–76

Trump, D. 1966. *Central and Southern Italy before Rome* (Thames & Hudson)

Tykot, R.H. & Andrews, T.K. (eds), *Sardinia in the Mediterranean: a footprint in the sea* (Sheffield Academic Press)

Webster, G.S. 1996. *A Prehistory of Sardinia 2300–500 BC* (Sheffield Academic Press)

SIX

THE AEGEAN

INTRODUCTION

In this chapter we consider the evidence for warfare in the Bronze Age Aegean, which includes mainland Greece, Crete and the Cycladic islands. During the Bronze Age sea travel around the Aegean and to other parts of the Mediterranean became possible, linking often distant lands and allowing a greater exchange of ideas and goods. The Bronze Age in the Aegean reflects a period of increasing prosperity in many areas, with the emergence of palaces, the production and trade of prestige goods, the adoption of writing and long-distance contacts with polities of the Near East and Egypt and, in the later Bronze Age, with the islands of the western Mediterranean.

Evidence for warfare in the Aegean comes in the form of man-made fortifications and the exploitation of naturally defended sites, weapons, iconography and funerary evidence ('warrior graves'), and the production of objects that symbolised warrior status (the warrior's panoply). In addition, the Aegean boasts two unique types of evidence in the form of written archives, notably the Linear B tablets, and the wall-paintings found on the island of Thera and at other sites on mainland Greece. These provide much important information about both warfare and warriors.

Theories on warfare have long been popular among Aegean scholars and have often formed explanations, or part explanations, for cultural changes, site destructions and Aegean-wide events. For example, warfare has been ascribed some role in the destructions taking place in the later part of the Early Bronze Age; in the emergence of the Minoan 'empire' in the Middle Bronze Age; in the appearance of palaces on mainland Greece; in the end of Knossian power; and in the series of events *c.* 1200 BC across the Aegean which caused disruption across much of the East Mediterranean. In the past, many scholars believed that major invasions from neighbouring regions could explain changes in material culture and site destructions, though such invasions were often difficult to substantiate. Warfare is also very much part of the mythological/literary traditions which survived through to the Classical period, especially in respect of the Trojan War. Greek literature is full of stories of conflicts both at sea and on land, with large-scale battles and sieges as well as heroic duels. In contrast to many other areas of Europe, the surviving Aegean evidence tends to represent the more symbolic or heroic aspects of warfare rather than the practical means of fighting and the functional use of weapons. Research into Bronze Age warfare in the Aegean has been strongly influenced by the images of fighting and duelling described in the Homeric epics and the rich burials within the shaft graves at Mycenae which both celebrate and glorify the heroes of war.

And the son of Atreus shouted his command to the Argives to buckle on their armour: and among them he himself armed in gleaming bronze. First he placed greaves on his legs, a fine pair, fitted with silver ankle-pieces. Next he put a corselet round his chest . . . over his shoulders he slung his sword: there were gold nails shining on it, and the scabbard sheathing it was of silver, attached to a baldric of gold. And he took up his mighty covering shield, a beautiful piece of intricate work which was plated with ten circles of bronze, and there were twenty bosses round it, white with tin, and at the centre of the plates one boss of dark blue enamel . . . The shield-strap was made of silver . . . And on his head he placed a four-bossed helmet, set round with horns, with a plume of horse-hair, . . . And he took up two strong spears, sharp-tipped with bronze, whose gleam struck far into the sky.

(*Iliad* II)

In this chapter we try to reconcile the two different types of warfare – the heroic/ceremonial side and the brutal reality of inter-group fighting.

THE NEOLITHIC AEGEAN

The earliest signs of warfare come from the Neolithic period. Although mainland Greece is characterised by broad regional contrasts in settlement types and locations, there are a small number of Neolithic sites in naturally defensive locations, or with good visibility of the surrounding area. Two Neolithic settlements in Thessaly (Sesklo and Magula Hadzimissiotiki) were surrounded by enclosure walls that were most probably defensive in nature and at Dimini the central area of the site was enclosed by a series of concentric stone walls (**Fig. 6.1**). At Emborio on the island of Chios the later Neolithic site was fortified. Recent evidence from Crete suggests that Late Neolithic fortified sites may have

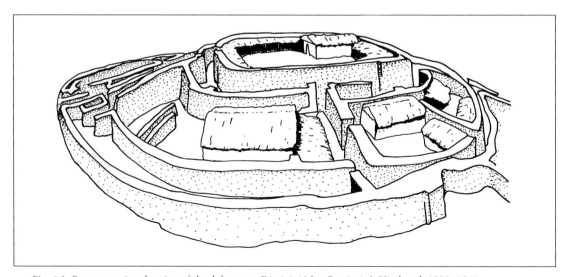

Fig. 6.1. Reconstruction drawing of the defences at Dimini. (After Preziosi & Hitchcock 1999: 186)

existed. There is very little evidence for weapons used specifically in fighting, as opposed to hunting, other than a few arrowheads and tanged points and clay sling-stones. In essence, it seems that there was little provision for the defence of settlements, and very few offensive weapons developed specifically for warfare. The most likely explanations for this are the rather fragmented settlement patterns, the lack of direct competition over resources and the absence of any sea-borne threat to the island and coastal communities.

THE BRONZE AGE

The Bronze Age covers a broad period between 3100/3000 to about 1100/1050 BC. Each phase of the Bronze Age has traditionally been divided into sub-phases based on regional and 'cultural' distinctions: Greece – Early, Middle and Late Helladic; Cyclades – Early, Middle and Late Cycladic; Crete – Early, Middle and Late Minoan. The Early Bronze Age covers the period between 3100/3000 and *c.* 2000 BC; the Middle Bronze Age begins around *c.* 2000 and finishes c. 1675/1650 BC; the end of the Bronze Age is around 1100–1050 BC. More specific dates for these sub-divisions largely rely on tracing connections between the Aegean and the more closely dated objects of the Near East and Egypt, and trying to reconcile these with the radiocarbon dates available. Over the years this has created many rival schemes (for a more detailed study of the chronology *see* Manning 1995: 217).

SETTLEMENTS AND FORTIFICATIONS

The Early Bronze Age period on mainland Greece saw the abandonment of many Neolithic sites, settlement expansion and the in-filling of many previously uninhabited areas. The population became increasingly nucleated in large centres, some of which were fortified. In Thessaly and the southern mainland nucleated settlements of 7–15ha are documented. The scattered Neolithic villages came together to form a 15ha settlement at Thebes and a 6ha site at Tiryns during the Early Bronze Age. (By the Late Bronze Age these had grown to *c.* 50 and *c.* 25ha respectively.) Halstead (1994) argues that since these large settlements are often associated with smaller neighbours, this may indicate the beginning of a settlement hierarchy. The Early Bronze Age also saw increased interaction and trade between regions and the emergence of large sites which acted as central storage and redistribution centres. It is also possible that these centres were developed for increased security, to counter the risk of crop failure and fend off attacks from other groups.

Artificial defences were constructed at several sites on the Greek coast during the Early Bronze Age, for example Manika, Aegina, Asketario and Lerna. In the Cyclades a number of sites were fortified around the middle of the Early Bronze Age and hilltop locations were also occupied. The presence of these fortified sites in coastal areas perhaps implies that danger was perceived as coming from the sea. The defences at Kastri and Aegina consisted of long narrow passages between stone walls, many leading to dead-ends to trap the attackers. This defensive strategy was previously used at the site of Dimini during the Neolithic. However, the walls at Kastri were not particularly thick or high (roughly

1m wide and possibly only 1.5m tall) and would easily have been breached under sustained attack, perhaps calling into question their defensive role. Natural and artificial defences are also found at the sites of Phylakopi, Siphnos and Koukounaries on the island of Paros. The inhospitable hilltop locations and defences at some of these sites suggest that they were designed to protect the site and its inhabitants, rather than being symbols of power and authority.

A number of these settlements were destroyed by burning at the end of the Early Bronze Age, for example the sites of Mallia, Myrtos and Vasiliki on Crete. Some areas of Crete were abandoned and more nucleated populations gathered in larger settlements although there was less disruption here than in other parts of the Aegean. Similar destructions occurred on the Cycladic islands; for example, the fortified site of Ayia Irini was damaged and the defences destroyed (but later repaired). The explanation for the phases of destruction seen on Crete and the Cyclades in the Early Bronze Age is still being debated and a natural phenomenon, such as a volcanic eruption or a period of climatic change, seems more likely than one involving human agents since such a wide area was affected. Sites on the Greek mainland were also destroyed and damaged by successive fires, as were Troy and other major sites in Anatolia (modern-day Turkey).

During the Middle Bronze Age massive stone enclosure walls were built at the site of Phylakopi, a double wall was constructed, connected by cross-walls and entered through gateways with specially thickened walls. A similar proliferation of defence-building can be seen in many other areas, continuing through to the Late Bronze Age. Fortified sites appeared in strategic locations such as at Malthi in Messenia. As far north as the area of Grevena there are signs of settlements built on naturally defensible sites. From the early Middle Bronze Age onwards the first true palaces were built on Crete, for example at Knossos, Phaistos, Mallia and Zakros (Demakopoulou 1999a). These sites comprised complexes of rooms, stores, archives, halls, corridors and courtyards and were endowed with beautiful wall-paintings. Although few of these sites are considered to have been fortified, there is a fine line between large stone walls designed as monumental statements and those which also included some defensive considerations – Knossos, for example, was enclosed by a stone wall. Many of these sites on Crete were destroyed in the mid-fifteenth century, although Knossos seems to have escaped unscathed.

Developments in the Late Bronze Age on the mainland, and especially in the Peloponnese, included massive 'Cyclopean' fortifications surrounding the hills where the palaces were constructed. These palaces were surrounded by offices, workshops and storerooms and housed an elite and their workforce. These sites across Greece include Nichoria, Mycenae, Pylos, Tiryns, Thebes, Orchomenos and Midea, built with 'imposing fortified citadels' (Demakopoulou 1999a: 67). The palace at Midea was built on a conical hill with strong natural defences and good visibility of the surrounding area. The fortification walls protected an inner citadel area with thick stone walls built in the Cyclopean style and defended by two stone gates (Demakopoulou & Divari-Valakou 1999).

The history of the development of Mycenae is one of increasing or progressive fortification. Major changes took place at Mycenae in the thirteenth century: the existing fortifications were extended and included walls up to 8m high, and a number of the earlier buildings, including Grave Circle A, were enclosed behind walls. The Lion

Fig. 6.2. The Lion Gate at Mycenae. (Photo: David Mason)

Gate with its projecting bastion was also constructed at this time (**Fig. 6.2**). This structure was designed to make the attackers vulnerable to counter-attack from those defending the entrance (Preziosi & Hitchcock 1999: 187–8). Similar bastions were found at other sites. The entrance at the site of Tiryns was approached via a ramp leading to a narrow passage with huge walls, 7–8m high and 5m thick, on either side (**Fig. 6.3**). The defences at sites such as Tiryns and Mycenae went far beyond what would have been required to keep out an enemy and this fact, and the monumental

Fig. 6.3. The entrance at Tiryns. (Photo: David Mason)

nature of the architecture, implies that these buildings were designed to confer great power and prestige on their owners.

There is much evidence to suggest that the Late Bronze Age was a period of intense competition and conflict in the Aegean. At many of the mainland sites fortifications were enlarged and strengthened, entrances were blocked off, walls and towers were added and rooms were converted to storage areas and workshops. The stock-piling of stones can be seen at Pseira: roughly a thousand stones were found, presumably ready to be used to pelt the enemy. At Mycenae, Tiryns and Athens a series of vaulted passages carried a water supply to the interior, perhaps in anticipation of groups laying siege to them (a similar feature is seen in Spain, see pp. 61–2). They were not to be disappointed. In the early thirteenth century some of the buildings at Mycenae were destroyed by fire. The excavator believed that oil had been deliberately poured into the basement of the House of the Oil Merchant to fuel the fire. Towards the end of the thirteenth and early twelfth centuries a series of destructions took place at various palaces and settlements, including the major citadels of Mycenae, Tiryns, Pylos and Nichoria, as well as many lesser sites. At the same time the Linear B tablets found in the palace at Pylos talk of making provisions for a potential danger coming from the sea (see below).

These destructions continued for many years and while large parts of the Greek mainland became depopulated, especially around western Attica, the Argolid, Messenia and Laconia, current survey data seems to suggest that other areas became more highly populated, especially the Cycladic islands and certain parts of the mainland.

The evidence therefore suggests that major changes took place in the Late Bronze Age on Crete, on some of the Cycladic islands and on the mainland, with the destruction of many palace sites and significant disruption to trade and interaction with other areas. Much of the Aegean was disrupted in some way which has led to speculation that the eruption of the Thera volcano, which occurred around this time, may be one explanation. Alternatively, the eruption may have weakened the social, economic and political structure of Minoan society which led in turn to the destruction and fall of the palaces. In a third explanation the Mycenaeans of mainland Greece are said to have 'invaded' Crete, removing local rulers and establishing a new social and political system. Whatever the true explanation, from here on society had a distinctly Mycenaean flavour, as reflected in the language in the Linear B writing system and in various objects and weapons from the mainland that were adopted into Minoan society.

The idea that the Minoans of Crete were a non-belligerent group of people comes largely from the subjects depicted in their frescoes and the supposed absence of fortifications on Crete at this time. In legend, the Minoans had a strong naval fleet and this, as well as the power and influence of King Minos and Crete's important trade links with other groups, may have been a deterrant to potential attackers from other islands or the mainland. Traditional arguments have considered that 'the Minoans' strength at sea was so great that they had no need to fortify their Cretan cities at all' (Castleden 1993: 162), although it is now clear that some of the major sites of the Early Bronze Age did have some defensive considerations, for example Pyros, Vasiliki, Debla and Ayia Photia. Many of the sites along the north coast, though lacking discernible artificial defences, occupied hilltop sites overlooking the sea. Sites such as Khamaizi could have functioned as effective look-out posts. Castleden also talks of 'psychological defences' in the form of the temple priestesses whose power was deemed to be a deterrent to looting and outbreaks of violent fighting (Castleden 1993: 163).

It is not clear how far Minoan influence stretched, although the artefactual evidence suggests the movement of people, raw materials and goods from Crete and within the Aegean in the Neolithic period and throughout the Bronze Age. Occurrences of Cretan pottery and other objects in distant parts of the Aegean, artistic influences and possible Minoan settlements abroad (Kastri on Kythera, Triandha on Rhodes and some on the Anatolian coast) suggest the presence of these trade links. It therefore seems more likely that some competition and fighting did exist on Crete and between Minoans and their neighbours, but that they chose not to depict it in their art, preferring instead to show aspects of nature and domestic scenes. As Castleden states, the idea that these were 'peace-loving' people may merely stem from an inaccurate or biased reading of the evidence.

BURIAL EVIDENCE

The burials of the Early Bronze Age tend to comprise multiple interments, either in isolated graves or as part of organised cemeteries. Some large cemeteries are documented from this period, especially in the Cyclades and on Crete (Demakopoulou 1999b: 99). The grave-goods deposited along with these burials and the degree of funerary ritual practised were dependent on the status of the individual(s). Although the grave-goods typically included weapons such as swords and daggers, no strong 'warrior symbolism' is seen in the burial evidence at this time.

More elaborate funerary monuments and richer grave offerings were seen in the Middle/Late Bronze Age with individual burials becoming much more common (as we saw in Spain in the Early Bronze Age). Very rich burials, such as Grave Circle B at Mycenae, and, before the end of the period, Grave Circle A, included many prestige objects as well as weapons, including foreign imports. Studies of the mortality profiles of burials from Mycenae and Pylos may indicate a high mortality rate for young adult males (Acheson 1999: 99). The individuals buried in the so-called 'warrior graves' were certainly strong, healthy men and their death in some form of conflict seems one possible explanation. The individuals buried in the shaft graves at Mycenae were accompanied by elaborately decorated weapons including inlaid daggers and swords, diadems, horse bits, a chariot model and high-status ceramic vessels. The presence of these weapons and other high-status items led to them being labelled 'warrior graves', although as we discussed in Chapter One, this does not necessarily mean they were actively engaged in fighting.

Large cemeteries containing rich burials were also found on Crete from the Early/Middle Bronze Age, apparently representing the wealth and status of a number of elite family groups. The 'warrior burials' at Knossos are equally striking for the quantity and nature of weapons they include. Likewise a series of Mycenaean graves from Achaea on the mainland contained a rich array of grave-goods including weaponry: the burial of a male adult at Kallithes-Spenzes contained a sword, bronze spearheads and a pair of bronze greaves. The latter are far from common and only accompanied high-ranking burials (*see* pp. 128–9). Although these burials are termed 'warrior graves', there is no evidence other than the presence of weaponry as grave-goods to confirm their belligerent role in society. Clearly by the Middle/Late Bronze Age the elite groups that occupied the palace sites were defining their status and position through prestige goods such as weapons. These objects certainly held great value for the living and were part of conspicuous consumption at the graveside.

PALAEOPATHOLOGY

There are only a small number of recorded examples of skeletal injuries and trauma most likely resulting from warfare from the Aegean area. Examples of cranial injuries come from Lerna and Asine (Arnott 1999) while at Mycenae a young male buried in Grave Circle A had been struck on the head by a sharp weapon, possibly a spear; he also had a healed wound from a previous violent encounter. Examples of parry fractures, especially to the forearms, were found on skeletal remains from Armenoi on Crete, along with other fractures and cut-marks (Arnott 1999).

Although skeletal remains have not always received much attention during excavations, the studies that have been carried out do provide some evidence for battle trauma. There is evidence for blows on the head from sharp weapons such as spears and arrows, but also perhaps from blunt tool/weapons such as axes and clubs.

WEAPONRY

The most notable change in weaponry from the Neolithic to the Bronze Age was the development from weapons used for hunting and adapted for fighting to those designed and produced specifically for inter-group warfare. The latter group can also be divided between weapons of purely practical value and those which have more ceremonial functions and were perhaps not designed, or in fact not suitable, to be used in actual combat.

Weaponry was undoubtedly an important part of Bronze Age society and weapons were traded between the Cycladic islands and the mainland, presumably for their prestige value. A large number of weapons were produced on Crete, which may seem surprising considering there are so few fortified sites and relatively little evidence for a belligerent society. Branigan (1999) estimates that around 15 per cent of metal production in Greece went into weapons, contrasting with a huge 80 per cent on Crete. While Peatfield (1999) argues that some of the Cretan daggers appear to have been damaged and changes in their design suggest that attempts were made to make them stronger and provide more support to the handler, he does not deny that they had great symbolic significance. Branigan on the other hand concludes that Cretan daggers were largely status symbols with many design features being more for show than practical use. In contrast, of the 230 daggers studied from the southern Aegean, the majority show some form of damage as a result of their use. The evidence therefore suggests a dual function for weapons, certainly during the Early Bronze Age, and this is most obvious in a comparison between Crete and the rest of the Aegean. The burials discussed above and the excavation of finds such as those discovered in a room at the site of Mallia on Crete (a sword, a dagger, a ceremonial axe-head and a longsword, the hilt of which was covered in sheet gold) confirm the importance of weapons in a social and ritual/ceremonial setting.

The daggers, swords and spears of the Early Bronze Age denote a change in tactics from the Neolithic, from distant, mobile fighting with projectiles to weapons 'designed for the close-quarter, unpredictable, multi-opponent confines of a mêlée' (Peatfield 1999: 72). 'We are led inescapably to the conclusion that EBI-II warfare was therefore almost entirely of a hand-to-hand nature' (Branigan 1999: 89), and this was certainly a matter of choice since other types of long-range weapons were available. At the site of Panormos on Naxos a pile of sling-stones was found outside the fortified gate which indicates that relatively 'primitive' weapons remained in use in the Bronze Age – baked clay examples date back to the Neolithic period. Sling-stones were also found at Kastri on the island of Syros. Spearheads were now made of bronze rather than stone, although they occur in relatively small numbers and were superseded by the dagger alongside changes in fighting styles. The disadvantages of making arrowheads/spearheads from bronze are their added weight and possible loss of aerodynamics, and the fact that they were more valuable than their stone equivalents.

The production of metal weapons truly takes off in the Late Early/Middle Bronze Age. A number of the swords found in the tombs at Mycenae (**Fig. 6.4**) have gold-plated handles and the mid-ribs are often decorated with scenes including animals in the hunt. Similar copper and silver examples are found on Crete. Differentiating between daggers

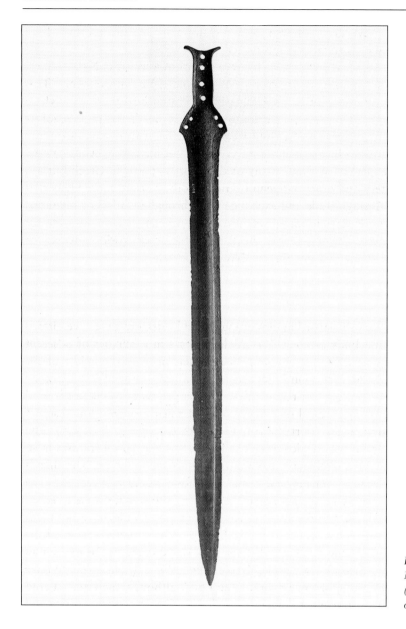

Fig. 6.4. Sword from the Mycenean acropolis. (Photo: National Museum of Athens)

and swords is often difficult and is largely determined by modern assumptions based on the length of the blade. Longer daggers were developed through the Middle Bronze Age which had a stronger mid-rib and were provisioned with a more secure attachment of the handle to the body. Swords were mainly used for hand-to-hand fighting, a thrusting weapon or rapier depicted as being aimed at the neck and shoulder area. The spear or javelin is frequently seen alongside the sword in many representations and is shown held with two hands and thrust forward on a horizontal plane. Also used in hunting, the short javelin could equally be used to 'hunt' charioteers very effectively. The warriors of the Late

Bronze Age had an impressive array of weapons, including spears and javelins, long swords and daggers, often with intricate designs and inlays.

One of the most significant introductions in the Late Bronze Age was the Naue Type II sword, which was the first slashing sword allowing 'cut-and-thrust' movements. This sword became widespread very quickly. Its place of origin is widely held to be somewhere in central Europe, although early examples are also found in northern Italy. Scholars disagree on how it reached the Aegean. The 'old views' are that invaders came from the Balkans, or that the swords were introduced via mercenaries, but increasing evidence now suggests a more peaceful explanation. Since many of the swords appear in Greek burials, associated with Greek pottery and other indigenous grave-goods, it seems more likely that the swords were acquired through trade and exchange than through invaders or migrants. Suffice to say that these swords revolutionised warfare in the Aegean, as Drews states, 'for the thirteenth century we have no long swords at all from the Greek world, whereas for the twelfth we have at least thirty of a single type' (Drews 1993: 204).

SHIELDS

The use of the spear/lance and the sword at close range would certainly have necessitated the provision of a shield and body armour. The shield appears in a number of different forms in Aegean iconography, including the large rectangular or 'tower' shield and the 'figure-of-eight' shield (**Fig. 6.5**). The Lion Hunt dagger from Shaft Grave IV at Mycenae shows three types of shield being used: rectangular, rectangular with a curved top and figure-of-eight (**Fig. 6.5**). An ivory model of a figure-of-eight shield was also found in the Mycenaean acropolis, dating to the fourteenth or thirteenth century BC (**Fig. 6.6**). The rectangular shield is most commonly depicted on Thera, and the few representations from Mycenae, Tiryns and Crete most likely stem from a Theran artistic influence. The shields are assumed to have been made from perishable materials for a number of reasons. The weight of the shield would clearly have been crucial in allowing the warrior some freedom of movement and shields of the size depicted in the iconography would have been too heavy if made from metal. Furthermore, details from the Theran wall-paintings suggest the actual materials that were used: the dappling of the shields suggests the use of ox hide in many cases, presumably stretched over a wooden frame. These shields would seem to have afforded good protection as they curved around the body, although their size would undoubtedly have made them somewhat cumbersome. In the Theran representations and the Lion Hunt dagger the shields appear to be held in place by a leather strap around the shoulder, leaving both hands relatively free.

A warrior vase from Mycenae from the end of the Late Bronze Age depicts six bearded warriors wearing horned helmets and body armour in the form of corselets and either leather or bronze greaves, and carrying a lance and a round shield (*see* **Fig. 6.8**). This vase shows that great changes had taken place in the warrior's panoply by this period. Smaller round shields were introduced in the Late Bronze Age. Drews argues that these smaller shields were used alongside thrusting spears and were designed for close fighting, giving the warrior greater freedom of movement than the earlier shield types. The central grip on the round shields was better designed to improve the mobility of the warriors.

Fig. 6.5. Depictions of different types of shield and weaponry. The lower illustration is the design on the Lion Hunt Dagger from Mycenae. (After Castleden 1993: 27, fig. 10)

HELMETS

Two main types of helmet are shown in the frescoes from Thera and in those from the mainland palace sites: the zoned padded leather helmet and the boar's tusk helmet (**Fig. 6.7**). The zoned helmet appears simultaneously on Crete, the Cyclades and at Mycenae although Knossos has been suggested as the origin of their distribution. Depictions of the boar's tusk helmet occur in significant numbers on the mainland and to a lesser extent on Thera and Crete. Although we cannot say for sure that these had a Mycenaean origin and were adopted by other groups, it is thought that boars were more likely to be present on the mainland than on any of the Aegean islands. Boar's tusk helmets have been much studied among Aegean archaeologists and a detailed description of their construction is given in the *Iliad*. Held on by leather chin-straps and sometimes with ear-guards, they were formed by overlaid tusks secured to a leather frame with thongs. The discovery of circular bone plume-holders in the Mycenaean shaft graves suggests that plumes were added to the top of the helmet, as represented on the frescoes. Fragments of gold tassels were also found at Mycenae which may have been part of the original plumes. It seems reasonable to assume that these plumes were indicative of status and/or group affiliation.

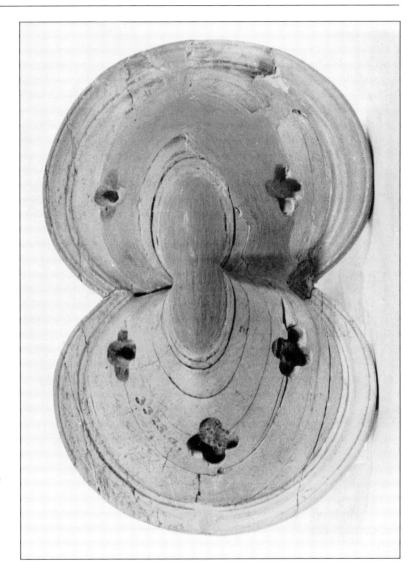

Fig. 6.6. Ivory model of a figure-of-eight shield from the Mycenean acropolis. (Photo: National Museum of Athens)

Another type of helmet that survives in the Knossian warrior graves is made completely of bronze (although this would surely have been impractical on the battlefield). The similarities in shape and form between this example and the boar's tusk helmets of the mainland suggests that this is a bronze imitation of a Mycenaean-style helmet. Some of these helmets also had cheek-pieces to protect the face and cheek-bones (*see* **Fig. 6.8**) and are associated with both boar's tusk and bronze helmets. Examples have been found at Sanatorion near Knossos, Eutresis and Eleusis in Greece, from Grave Circle B at Mycenae and from Dendra. These cheek-pieces share many affinities with similar types from all over continental Europe.

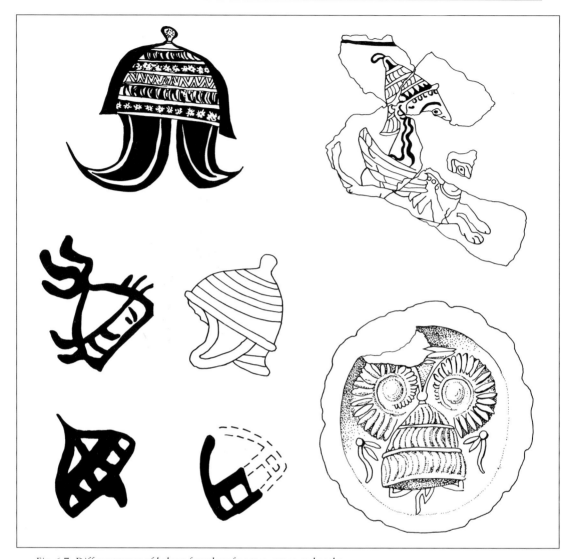

Fig. 6.7. Different types of helmet found on frescoes, vases and sealstones.

CORSELETS AND GREAVES

Pieces of armour are occasionally found in the archaeological record, like the famous corselet found at Dendra, but are frequently seen in the frescoes and Late Bronze Age pictorial *kraters* (*see* below). The corselets of the Early/Middle Bronze Age were principally reserved for charioteers and appear to have been made of leather. The Dendra corselet was made completely of bronze and although some have argued that it was designed for an infantryman, its size (reaching the knees) and weight would have rendered him immobile and therefore useless on the battlefield. The corselets of the Late Bronze Age, as depicted in frescoes and on vases, were much less cumbersome and were made

Fig. 6.8. Detail of a warrior from the Late Bronze Age 'Warrior Krater'.

either of leather or material with metal strips attached (**Fig. 6.8**). Greaves are also seen in the iconography and appear in the burials of the later period. Examples have been found: at Dendra a single greave was found in the Cuirass Tomb, while fragments of decorated greaves were found in tombs at Kallithea in Achaea. Again, Drews argues that the introduction of armour such as corselets and greaves ties in with changes in weaponry and changes in fighting tactics, affording better protection for the infantryman (*see* below).

Fig. 6.9. Detail of a warrior from the Thera miniature fresco, 'Assembly on Hill'.

ICONOGRAPHY

The Aegean has two important categories of evidence for the study of warfare that are not found elsewhere in Europe: frescoes and written tablets. The frescoes, stelae, seals and painted ceramic vessels show a familiarity with warriors and fighting, albeit often in a symbolic or ceremonial setting. They depict armed men on foot and in chariots, wearing helmets, corselets and greaves and carrying shields, swords and spears, many of which are found in the burials of the period. The iconographic evidence also sometimes provides clues as to the identity of aggressors.

Warriors, their weapons and particular scenes or events were portrayed in the wall-paintings of Thera. They include lines of armed foot soldiers and 'naval battles' (**Fig. 6.9**), with men swirling helplessly in the water. The great attention paid to the detail of the helmets, weapons, shields and dress of the warriors provides an invaluable insight into warfare in this period. The Theran scenes show the sword and spear as the main weapons. Swords are not shown in use and the majority are seen projecting below shields, therefore it is assumed that they were attached at the waist and held in a scabbard. The spear frequently occurs alongside the sword, which supports the evidence from the grave finds discussed earlier. In the frescoes the spears often appear to be more than twice the height of the figures and therefore they should perhaps be termed javelins. Most often they are depicted as long thin poles without a spearhead at the end, although we know from the grave finds that spearheads were used.

A belligerent society is depicted in the art of the Mycenaeans with scenes of men and animals fighting portrayed on rings and seal-stones, for example on a gold seal-bead from Circle A at Mycenae. The warrior goddess is a recurrent theme in much of the iconography. She is often seen brandishing a sword and carrying a figure-of-eight shield. This type of shield also appears in much Mycenaean and Minoan art, especially on frescoes from the palaces at Knossos, Tiryns and Thebes and at Mycenae. Another important group of scenes is found on the funerary stelae of the shaft graves of Circles A and B at Mycenae. In addition, the silver *rhyton* from Circle A shows two groups of warriors, while another from the same circle shows a town under siege, with men and boats and defending archers. Among the small number of bellicose scenes from the Pylos frescoes is a duel between a figure wearing greaves, a boar's tusk helmet and a short white tunic and wielding a dagger, and an opponent wearing an animal skin but bare legs and also armed with a dagger. It is thought that this scene represents a Mycenaean warrior fighting a 'barbarian'. An illustrated papyrus from Amarna, now in the British Museum, shows a group of warriors, some with boar's tusk helmets, although they wear Egyptian loincloths rather than Aegean costumes. Whether this suggests that warriors from the Aegean served in Egypt at the time of Akhenaten, or whether Aegean symbols of warrior status were adopted by the Egyptians, remains unclear.

Chariots are widely depicted in Egyptian and Near Eastern art, and in the Aegean from the later Bronze Age. The Aegean evidence is derived from depictions on grave stelae, the most famous example coming from Grave Circle A at Mycenae (**Fig. 6.10**) and from later vase paintings and conjectural evidence from the Linear B tablets (*see* below). The 'megaron frieze' from Mycenae shows the preparations for battle, the horses being attended to and fighting scenes involving horse-drawn chariots. Representations of chariots in motion are found on seal-stones, for example one from the tholos tomb at Vapheio, where an armed warrior is shown on the chariot. Two lightly armed warriors with helmets and spears, one of them on a chariot, are shown on a fresco from the palace of Pylos.

Much debate surrounds the actual function of chariots and the degree to which they were directly involved in battles. Homer mentions that chariots were used for transportation to and from the battlefield rather than as fighting platforms, which led many people to argue that chariots were either for transportation or were prestigious items that conveyed status and wealth, whether in real terms or when depicted in the iconography (*see* below). Although much of the terrain over which they were fighting

Fig. 6.10. Different forms of chariot: (a) the Pylos fresco; (b) Kamid El-Loz, Lebanon; (c) Mycenae.

would have been hilly, there were also flat plains where chariots could have been effectively used in battle. The stele from Mycenae shows a figure armed with a sword riding in a chariot, either for sport or in battle, with another armed figure ahead of him. Pictorial *kraters* from the Late Bronze Age onwards also depict chariots alongside armed men wearing helmets, corselets and greaves and holding shields, spears and swords.

WARFARE AT SEA

It should be no surprise that conflict also took place at sea. Boats, and warrior figures in boats, are common themes in the iconography of the Bronze Age Aegean, a society that depended on sea travel for much of its trade and transfer of people and ideas. The logistics of sea travel in this period have been widely studied and it seems clear that for many of the smaller populated settlements it would not have been possible to man large vessels or to travel large distances. In the Early Bronze Age only a handful of Cycladic sites practised long-distance trade and it is from these sites that we primarily find 'foreign' prestige goods, for example Kastri on Syros and Ayia Irini on Keos. Therefore, raiding trips between the southern Cycladic islands and from these islands

Fig. 6.11. A Late Bronze Age krater sherd from Kynos depicting a warship. (After Demakopoulou et al. 1999: 201, fig. 2)

to mainland Greece and Anatolia, and vice versa, would have been feasible only for a small number of groups. However, the fortified sites built on the coastal shores of many of the islands and the mainland suggest that the frequency of these exchanges rose during the Bronze Age, whereas their absence on Crete may suggest that this island was still largely beyond reach.

Branigan (1999: 87) talks of 'aggressive looking long-boats'. Boats, often containing warriors, are depicted on Mycenaean and Theran wall-paintings. Though some of these depictions could represent the transportation of warriors, others clearly show sea battles. The Theran 'shipwreck' scene shows a damaged boat, and shields and warriors in the water. Belligerent ships are also depicted on a series of *kraters* from the Late Bronze Age. The ships largely take the form of oared galleys with a helmsman, and warriors lined up within the main body of the boat. The development of the oared galley 'may justifiably be considered the single most significant advance in the weaponry of the Bronze Age Eastern Mediterranean' (Wedde 1999: 465). Wedde argues that the principal tactical advantages of this type of vessel are its speed when rowed and its ability to be beached on to land at speed. The Livanates *krater* shows two ships opposing each other as if in a sea battle – this is the first example of this type of scene, although the fresco scenes imply the same. The *krater* sherd from Kynos in Greece shows a nine-oared boat with two warriors fighting on deck, a further figure at the helm and another at the front of the boat, clearly defined by his plumed helmet (**Fig. 6.11**). The two fighting warriors are differentiated by their shields: one has a round shield of the sort described above, the other is a 'Hittite-shape' shield.

LINEAR B ARCHIVES

The Linear B tablets are a series of archives recorded on clay tablets found at a number of palace sites including Knossos, Pylos, Mycenae, Tiryns and Khania. Among other things, they provide information on the production and issue of weapons, rationing, the deployment of troops and the use of mercenaries (Palaima 1999). They also include inventories of the number and condition of the chariots and their equipment, the horses that drew them, and the weapons and other accoutrements of the warriors. The 'Sa' tablet from Pylos, for example, refers to the number of chariot wheels in both good and bad state of repair. The Knossos Sg1811 tablet has an inventory of 246 chariot frames and 208 pairs of wheels. The tablets also contain references to names such as 'he who kills', 'he who is quick in battle' and has terms for 'military' and 'warrior'. Although they do not record historic events or those involved in fighting, they show an awareness of the infrastructure required for organised conflict and the provision of arms suggesting an ever-present aggressor. The palaces were the production and distribution centres for arms and armour and presumably held the power and authority over those who fought.

CONCLUSIONS

The iconography is perhaps the most important aspect of the Aegean evidence since it not only gives an indication of what types of weaponry and armour were in use, but also provides some idea as to how they were used and by whom. However, the artistic evidence also raises problems concerning what was being represented, and whether we should view these scenes as historically accurate or whether they represent a more idealised picture of warfare, perhaps a Homeric-type ideology. As we have discussed throughout this chapter, there is much archaeological evidence to support the imagery on wall-paintings, seals and other media, although again this largely comes from burials which do not reflect the ordinary warrior, the low-status members of society who undoubtedly served in the front line. There is much conflicting evidence as to the functional versus social/ceremonial use of many aspects of Bronze Age warfare. Were many of the weapons purely for show? Do the wall-paintings show real battles between distinct groups or do they describe an idealised world or hypothetical victories over enemies and ceremonial shows of strength and power? Were the monumental 'cyclopean' citadels and palaces functional fortresses, or were they largely for show? How can we reconcile these opposing aspects of the evidence?

Depictions of warriors on land and at sea are preserved in wall-paintings, on seals, ceramics and other artistic media. Warriors are shown marching, presumably to battle, travelling in boats, drowning at sea and dying on land. Bronze Age warriors are typically seen fighting at close-quarters, and many have distinctive attributes, such as particular types of clothing or weapons and armour, suggesting that identity and social affiliation were very important. Some of the scenes have a real sense of 'them' and 'us' – or 'Mycenaean' and 'non-Mycenaean'. It is clear throughout the Bronze Age that the warrior's panoply was of great social importance in conveying prestige and power, in addition to its functional advantages. Lyvia Morgan (1988) suggests that the nakedness of many figures in the shipwreck scene was used to identify the defeated; if correct, it was undoubtedly a powerful message.

It should be reiterated that Crete is often atypical. The large numbers of weapons, especially daggers, produced in the Early/Middle Bronze Age does not necessarily mean that warfare was on the increase and that the tactics of fighting had changed. Many have argued that a large number of these weapons were for ceremonial use and their major function was as grave-goods. Comparing daggers from the mainland and Crete, it certainly seems that the aesthetic appearance of the dagger was imitated on Crete perhaps without the appropriate knowledge of the hafting process, and without understanding why certain techniques were used to ensure a strong joint between the blade and haft. We assume a relatively low level of conflict on Crete during much of the Bronze Age based on slight evidence for the fortification of sites and little palaeopathological evidence for battle injury and trauma, although this picture of a non-belligerent society may be obscured by this lack of evidence and by the portrayal of Minoan society on the frescoes.

Crete is the most southerly island in the Aegean and its distance from the mainland and other islands perhaps protected it from the advances of other groups. The availability of boats and the advent of sea travel created not only opportunities for moving goods and people around the Aegean, but also the conditions for piracy.

Elsewhere in the Aegean, weaponry and artificial defences were much more functional than on Crete and can be regarded as a response to real threats and insecurities. However, the actual defensive structures were technically and tactically less sophisticated than many of their counterparts in other areas of Europe. The evidence of continued destructions and fires at many of the major sites shows an inability or unwillingness to find ways of countering these attacks or natural disasters (*see* below).

On the mainland and in the Cyclades we find evidence for the functional use of weapons, developments in weapon technology towards greater efficiency and effectiveness, and the building of defences which were designed to keep out the enemy, as well as to symbolise power and status. Evidence for the use of archery comes from iconographic evidence, examples of arrowheads and the adoption of bastions at some sites. Sling-stones are also attested in this period at a small number of sites and may have been a very useful defensive weapon. Homer suggests that they were an effective measure against an attacking force:

> . . . the troops on the wall above, who kept up a barrage of stones flung from the well-built battlements, . . stones showered to the ground like snowflakes . . . and helmets and bossed shields rang hollow as rocks huge as mill-stones crashed on to them.
>
> (*Iliad* 12)

In this regard, defensive walls, bastions and towers would then have been needed to give the defenders a height advantage over the attackers, as well as providing a protective barrier around the settlement or citadel.

However, it seems more likely that, as Branigan concludes, this must surely mean that Aegean societies were imitating structures from other areas and other groups who used different methods of fighting. Clearly archery was known and practised in the Aegean, especially for hunting, and therefore we must assume that the decision not to use it in inter-group fighting was one of choice. It is not clear whether other types of weapon (swords, daggers, spears) were produced or copied from ideas practised elsewhere and their adoption led to changes in the fighting tactics, or whether the need for close-combat weapons led to the adoption and modification of the new bronze weaponry. Whatever the answer, weapons performed a dual function from very early on in their existence. Anthropomorphic stelae and menhir depictions from the Early Bronze Age of northern Greece suggest that the dagger was already a male-specific object and was perhaps part of a group of objects that signified status and perhaps rank. The rich array of weapons and defensive armour from burials across the Aegean undeniably speaks of the high social regard for these objects in representing status and authority. Since access to some of these objects, such as greaves and boar's tusk helmets, was not available to everyone, these objects must have demarcated the elite within society. Access to 'exotic' objects, materials and knowledge, especially from beyond the Aegean, meant that trade and sea travel were of major importance, and created competition and conflict among the elite groups whose position and credibility relied on the acquisition of these goods and on the ability to out-compete their rivals.

The overall impression of Aegean Bronze Age society is of one well versed in weaponry and warfare, but which, initially at least, lacked technical competence. Although good imitators of foreign ideas, they often lacked the technical understanding of advances in defence-building and weapon technology devised elsewhere. Whether this is because Aegean societies were less belligerent or simply because they practised a very different form of fighting is not clear. Clearly the burial record and iconography provide insights only into elite warfare and warriors and it may be that we have not yet uncovered the evidence relating to the ordinary warrior, his weaponry and armour, and the more mundane and brutal aspects of the battlefield. For a slightly romanticised version of such events, we hand over to Homer and the clash between the Achaians and Trojans:

> When they had advanced together to meet on common ground, then there was the clash of shields, of spears and the fury of men cased in bronze: bossed shields met each other, and the din rose loud. Then there were mingled the groaning and the crowing of men killed and killing, and the ground ran with blood.
>
> (*Iliad* 8)

THE END OF THE BRONZE AGE

Many questions surround the fate of the Bronze Age societies in the Aegean. Who or what destroyed so many of the palatial sites and why were they not rebuilt? What caused the Mycenaean kingdoms to collapse? Why did the Cycladic culture die out? The whole of the East Mediterranean was in turmoil at the end of the Bronze Age.

One proposed explanation is that the 'Sea Peoples' invaded and caused the destructions. Historical records from the East Mediterranean provide evidence on raids, sea-battles and also the eventual victory of the army of Egypt over the 'Sea Peoples', although their identity and historical validity remains undefined. One of the most innovative explanations that has arisen in recent times is that of Robert Drews (1993). His argument takes in much of the evidence we have discussed for the Late Bronze Age: the destruction of many sites by fire; a dependence on chariot warfare by the kingdoms of the Aegean; changes in weaponry and the defensive panoply geared more towards the infantryman than the charioteer; and evidence of changes taking place in other parts of Europe. Drews argues that a new style of warfare emerged at the end of the Bronze Age, accompanied by new types of weapons (the javelin and sword), smaller round shields, greaves and corselets. For him, these developments reflect the shift from traditional chariot-based warfare to a new style of guerrilla fighting based on an army of infantrymen. 'A contrast emerges, it seems, between warfare against civilized enemies and warfare against men from the hinterland, whom I shall call barbarians' (Drews 1993: 138). Ultimately, he argues that these changes enabled the Bronze Age kingdoms to be defeated by discontented barbarians.

After the end of the Bronze Age the archaeological and literary record is fairly silent on the nature of warfare and we must rely on evidence from other areas, such as Assyria (see Drews 1993: 164–8). What is clear is that the type of warfare practised in the Late Bronze Age was radically transformed by the introduction and widespread adoption of infantry in the Early Iron Age. Depictions on Geometric vases, evidence from burials and literary descriptions such as those of Homer, announce this change and attest to the general embracing of mass infantries arranged in the phalanx (a line of foot soldiers). 'Thus chariot warfare, which in the Late Bronze Age had distinguished cities and kingdoms from the barbarous hinterlands (where horses and chariot were a luxury that few, if any, could afford), did not survive into the Iron Age, and even the wealthiest kings had now to depend primarily upon footsoldiers' (Drews 1993: 165).

FURTHER READING

Laffineur, R. (ed.). 1999. *Aegaeum 19: Polemos, Le Contexte Guerrier en Egée a l'Age du Bronze* (Univ. de Liège)

Castleden, R. 1993. *Minoans. Life in Bronze Age Crete* (Routledge)

Dickinson, O. 1994. *The Aegean Bronze Age* (Cambridge University Press)

Drews, R. 1993. *The End of the Bronze Age. Changes in warfare and the catastrophe ca. 1200 BC* (Princeton University Press)

Preziosi, D. & Hitchcock, L.A. 1999. *Aegean Art and Architecture* (Oxford University Press)

SEVEN

CONCLUSIONS

All the preceding chapters have presented convincing evidence that warfare was a widespread and lethal phenomenon experienced by peoples of the Bronze Age throughout Europe. As we have shown, we have more than just weapons and fortifications at our disposal to inform us about patterns of prehistoric warfare, and far-reaching conclusions can be reached from studying a range of different pieces of evidence. A comparative approach, such as taken in this book, allows us to compare and contrast the evidence from different areas of Europe during the same period. Thus, where certain types of evidence are lacking or difficult to interpret in some areas, material from other regions may suggest explanations for this. For example, well-preserved evidence for textiles, perishable weapons and objects from the warrior's panoply in northern Europe suggest what types of evidence are missing from more arid areas such as Spain. This comparative approach also provides us with a firmer point of reference when interpreting representations of weaponry and armour in rock carvings and paintings since evidence from other areas may suggest how the depictions may be interpreted differently. But a comparative approach allows us to go much further than merely 'filling in the gaps' in this way; for example, it allows us to identify more general patterns of warfare, to find instances where the offensive and defensive strategies adopted were similar (and where they differed), and to see how innovations in weapon technology spread and were adopted alongside existing traditions across a wide area.

The modern countries of Europe have been used to divide the chapters for ease of presentation; clearly, though, such divisions did not exist in prehistory. Contact between areas facilitated the spread of beliefs, ideas and goods, especially as a result of trade. In many respects the various areas of Europe are very different in terms of the development of warfare; this can largely be explained by their geographical isolation and/or the persistence of existing local traditions. The importance of geography at this time cannot be over-emphasised. For example, for much of the Bronze Age groups in Spain progressed along their own line of development relatively isolated from the rest of Europe; it was not until the later Bronze Age, when trade links were extended and groups were moving more regularly to and from the Iberian peninsula, that Spain assumed many of the ideas and traditions seen in other areas (notably, in this case, from central Europe via southern France). The same is true of the Aegean. The location of the Cyclades, Crete and mainland Greece is a crucial factor in explaining the nature and development of warfare. For example, Crete's remote position in the southern Aegean meant that for much of the Bronze Age the Minoans appear to have enjoyed a very peaceful existence, until contact was made with the Cycladic islands and the mainland (principally through trade initially). In contrast, the Cyclades were obviously threatened by groups from the mainland much earlier in the Bronze Age which resulted in the construction of coastal defended sites and necessitated changes in the nature and efficiency of weaponry. The reverse may also be true – people on the islands might have wanted resources only available on the mainland or on other islands – and they might have obtained them either by peaceful trade or by raiding and pillaging.

In central and northern Europe there seem to have been much closer links between groups and more regular movement of people, transferring objects and materials as well as ideas and knowledge.

Having emphasised the differences in the forms of warfare practised across some areas of Europe, arguing that perhaps these are due to geographical and topographical factors, there also exist some surprising similarities between distant regions. One obvious example of this is the 'V' or 'U-shaped' notch found on many shields, and in depictions of shields from Spain, Britain and across central Europe. Although this feature is likely to be largely functional, perhaps denoting which way up the shield is to be held (where the handle/strap is), this does not explain why such distant groups adopted the same means of showing this. As with many other aspects of Bronze Age weaponry and the warrior's panoply, it is not clear whether these similarities are to be interpreted as different people making the same response to the same problems, or whether we should be looking for evidence of contacts and stylistic exchange between groups earlier than is currently acknowledged.

The period referred to as the 'Bronze Age' differs in calendar years BC from area to area. Given this caveat, were the patterns of conflict, types of weaponry, and modes of defence uniform throughout Bronze Age Europe?

WARFARE AT THE START OF THE BRONZE AGE

Archery

At the start of the Bronze Age, it seems that archery was of huge importance, at least in terms of warfare. There are a number of facets to this: archery was presumably frequently used to hunt animal prey, but was also used to fight humans, and in the Beaker Period the portrayal of the individual as a warrior with archer's equipment was essential in burial rites. Bows are known to have been used from the Mesolithic period onwards and the dominance of this type of weaponry appears to be almost total throughout the majority of our study regions at the dawn of the Bronze Age.

Arrows were used in attacks on Neolithic sites in northern and western Europe. The work of Roger Mercer at Hambledon Hill in Dorset has shown that stone arrowheads were the direct cause of death of an individual in the Stepleton enclosure at the site. At Crickley Hill in Gloucestershire arrowheads remained around the defences of the site which was subsequently burnt down, probably as a direct result of attack. A bone projectile point was found embedded in the nose, and a further, fatal, point in the chest of a man recovered from the Neolithic site of Pormose in Denmark. In the west, in the period between the Neolithic and height of the Early Bronze Age, many burials beneath barrows are found to be accompanied by arrowheads, archer's wristguards and a ceramic Beaker (which gave the period its name). The burial tradition was not simply designed to give an artificial portrayal of the inhumed individual as an archer; several bodies reflect the fact that the deceased had been directly affected by archery. Bodies buried at Stonehenge and Barrow Hills in England may have been killed by arrow wounds.

The famous rock art of Scandinavia includes several depictions of warriors armed with bows, an image mirrored by the statues from Petit Chasseur in Switzerland. These statues seem to depict warriors clad in quilted armour (which was particularly effective against archery) and holding bows. In central and eastern Europe arrowheads of bone, stone and bronze are found in numerous burial contexts. At both Klings and Stetten in Germany arrowheads were found still embedded in excavated corpses.

The situation regarding archery in Italy is similar to that in much of the rest of Europe. In the Copper Age barbed and tanged arrowheads were placed in burials, as they were in the Early Bronze Age, but their prescence declined in the archaeological record during the Middle Bronze Age. Perhaps our best example of Copper Age archery is the extraordinary discovery of the Iceman from the Alps, who was carrying a bow and arrows. Astonishingly, as well as his quiver, the fletching of the arrowshafts and even the substances used to fix the projectile heads to the arrowshafts were recovered. It is probable that the Iceman's type of bow and accompanying equipment differed little into the Early Bronze Age. Although there is little physical evidence for the importance of archery in the Late Bronze Age, an interesting dichotomy exists in that a series of Nuraghic warrior statues, with bows, *have* been found. Dating from the eleventh to seventh centuries BC, these figures appear to be wearing leather armour and helmets, and some have shields as well.

In Iberia flint arrowheads were used in hunting and fighting during the Neolithic and Copper Age, and they continued to be used alongside metal versions in the early Bronze Age. A number of examples of skeletal injuries as a result of embedded arrowheads are found in these periods, and the presence of defensive bastions and walls with small 'openings' confirms the use of archery. The appearance of archer's wristguards as part of the Beaker package provides further evidence, and indicates the need to improve the efficiency of the weapons.

The Aegean seems, perhaps, to differ from much of the rest of Europe, perhaps as a result of its topographic make-up as a series of islands. Although obsidian arrowheads are known, it appears that the bow was perhaps less significant here than in the rest of Europe. Based upon current evidence it appears that in this region daggers and spears were dominant.

Daggers

Although almost no skeletons with dagger wounds have been found, or at least none recognised as such, this weapon was also an important part of the warrior panoply at the start of the Bronze Age. These early blade weapons were important prestige objects, found in high-status burials throughout Europe and depicted in the iconography of Scandinavia, Valcamonica and Monte Bego in Italy and on the weapons stelae of Iberia. In the Aegean, the relative scarcity of arrowheads and the presence of daggers have been interpreted as an indication of a different style of warfare in this region, at much closer range and, although arrowheads are found later in the Bronze Age, this may also be true for continental Europe as the period progresses. In addition to bows and arrows and daggers, axes and halberds may also have been used in some engagements.

Defensive Equipment

In terms of body protection, much of the panoply available to the Bronze Age warrior really appears later in the Bronze Age. However, the representations of quilted armour by the statue stelae at Petit Chasseur appear to indicate that some defensive equipment was utilised, possibly in response to the use of bows and arrows in combat. A wooden shield-former, which was used as a mould for the construction of leather shields, found at Kilmahamogue in Ireland has recently been radiocarbon dated to 1950–1540 BC. This would suggest that shields were in use at quite an early stage in the Bronze Age in western Europe, a situation almost certainly mirrored in east and central Europe (and probably in the Aegean, Iberia and Italy).

Shields were not designed for use against arrows; rather they were intended to protect against blows at close range, perhaps from daggers. This clearly represents a break from the longer-range bow and arrow combat which was perhaps superseded as the dominant form of combat at quite an early phase of the Bronze Age, even though arrow-use did not disappear entirely.

Fortifications

Can the earlier settlements and fortifications add to this picture of combat? Well, for much of Europe substantial defensive structures appear in larger numbers in the Urnfield Period, linked to the exchange networks of the day. Perhaps the most striking aspect of the Spanish evidence, when compared to other areas, is that the fortified sites appearing in the Copper Age were among the earliest in Europe and their defensive structures were developed locally in response to local conditions. In other words, they were not influenced by ideas, technologies or building types from continental Europe. Here we see the adoption and development of defensive structures responding to local needs for protection within a hostile environment. The investment of time, materials and labour in these structures throughout the Copper and Bronze Ages suggests that inter-group fighting was present within society and perhaps was an everyday part of it. Many of the defences were vast undertakings for a local population and required planning and long-term investment in their maintenance and repair. The building techniques adopted and the types of defensive structures created changed somewhat in the Bronze Age and were geared towards greater efficiency and effectiveness, with groups opting for locations and constructions that reduced the amount of investment required. Unlike some other areas of Europe, the evidence from Spain suggests that the earliest defended sites were ultimately practical and functional, while also being impressive monuments.

At the start of the Bronze Age central/eastern Europe was dotted with fortified tells and nucleated villages with ditches and banks, often located close to natural resources. The defences often utilise natural elements of the landscape to provide protection. The phenomenon of large defended structures really takes off in the Urnfield Period. A similar situation exists in western Europe despite the fact that 'hillforts' of a type existed in the Neolithic (and there is even evidence for attacks on some of them). Several Italian fortified sites, some with multiple walls, also had their origins in the Neolithic. A number of sites in north-east Italy were founded in around the eighteenth century BC and may have stayed in use until the Roman period!

In the Early Bronze Age of the Aegean some settlements were fortified and populations became increasingly nucleated in large centres following the abandonment of Neolithic sites. Like the Copper Age sites of Iberia, early sites were defended both with walls and with towers. For example, Kastri had substantial defences including passages designed to lead into a dead-end to confuse would-be attackers. The locations of these sites and the scale of their defences suggest that they were functional; indeed, some sites appear to have been burned down at the end of the Early Bronze Age.

SUMMARY

At the start of the Bronze Age it appears that the bow and arrow was initially the most important weapon, necessitating the design of defended settlements to counter the threat they posed. Although bows remained in use, the emergence of a short bladed weapon, the dagger, was of huge importance in that it perhaps indicates changes in combat styles, moving from the (relatively) long-distance projectile-based fighting of archery, utilising the speed and agility of the warrior, to closer-range combat with heavier side-arms. Other elements from the end of the early period provide similar evidence for this change. The Kilmahamogue shield-former has a later Early/early Middle Bronze Age origin and points to the use of shields at an early stage in the Bronze Age. This form of defence was of greatest use against bladed weapons or spears at close quarters.

WARFARE IN THE MIDDLE AND LATE BRONZE AGE

Weaponry

Our dataset for the Middle Bronze Age is perhaps more limited than that for both the Early and Late periods because in many cases the burial rites are in the form of cremation, but even so enough information is available to enable us to draw broad conclusions. Spears begin to appear at the end of the Early Bronze Age and are firmly established as the main projectile weapon by the Middle Bronze Age. It is difficult to differentiate between 'thrusting' and 'throwing' spears, and studies based solely on lengths and widths of spearheads in order to distinguish between uses of spear are too simplistic. Shorter (and thus traditional 'throwing') spears would have been just as deadly when used in a thrusting fashion – as some of the palaeopathological material reveals. This being said, spears may have replaced arrows as the dominant projectile type by the Middle Bronze Age, being objects of great prestige as well as of clear utility.

Daggers have been found throughout Middle Bronze Age Europe, including elegant silver and copper daggers from the Aegean. As the period developed the blade weapons increased in length from short (dagger) to long (rapiers and leaf-shaped swords). Although all these weapon groups were used in close-quarter fighting, the manner of their use was very different. The dagger of the Early Bronze Age and the later rapiers were both stabbing weapons, but the latter was far more difficult to use successfully. These finely crafted objects had a relatively thin blade and their use would have required at least some training: the long stabbing action is not as natural a technique as a sweeping slash. The general opinion is that warriors using the rapier would have met on a one-to-one level – as 'champions'. With the emergence of these blade weapons used by champions, protective equipment, projecting further prestige upon the user, was perhaps more widespread. The Aegean Middle/Late Bronze Age appears blessed with dramatic protective equipment such as probable leather body armour, greaves, helmets and so-called 'tower' shields, while its settlements were defended by massive stone enclosures with cross-walls and gateways with reinforced walls, often on naturally defensible locations.

The blades of Middle Bronze Age weapons frequently reveal tears around the rivet holes at the top of the blade handles, indicating that they had been used in a sweeping fashion, damaging the rapier. The appearance of swords with slashing attributes negated this problem. The leaf-shaped swords of the later Bronze Age were beautiful, prestigious objects requiring much skill and metalworking knowledge to make. They, too, were of practical use and many such objects seem to reveal nicks along their edges consistent with their use in combat. Technology had advanced far enough by this time to be able to produce a sword with both slashing and stabbing attributes: the Carp's Tongue swords (Ewart Park variants) of the Late Bronze Age. The distribution of these swords – they are found along the Atlantic coastlines of southern Britain, northern France and Iberia – hints at strong links between these regions.

Fortifications

Our evidence for combat and for styles of warfare is greatly enhanced in the Late Bronze Age. Hillforts emerge at the end of the Middle Bronze Age in Central Europe, and in the Urnfield Period these seem to be many and varied. The fortifications enclose much domestic activity and in many cases the production of prestige goods. These agrarian settlements are found on trade-routes along rivers and sea-routes that had developed as the Bronze Age progressed. In addition to these large-scale fortified sites on high ground, lower-lying sites are sometimes provided with defences too. However, evidence for attacks against these sites is sparse – perhaps the results of such an engagement are visible in the archaeological record at Blucina, though this is far from being unequivocal (*see* p. 69). This situation is mirrored in the northern and western regions. Perhaps the larger defended sites emerged here at a slightly later date than their eastern counterparts, but by the Late Bronze Age high-lying sites were often fortified. The Neolithic sites of Crickley Hill and Hambledon Hill may both have been stormed, but until the Late Bronze Age there is no parallel in terms of evidence for attack. At Tormarton, bodies with spearheads embedded within them were thrown into a ditch without ceremony (*see* p. 21). It is possible that this was the enclosure ditch of a low-lying fortified settlement, and that the bodies were those of men killed during an attack, though work on this site is incomplete.

In Spain, many of the fortified sites of the Early and Middle Bronze Age continued to be occupied although the defences frequently fell into disrepair and many were abandoned by the end of the period. The great *floruit* of the heavily fortified settlement had ended. The Late and Final Bronze Age in Italy were characterised by settlement disruption in many areas and depopulation in others. This was perhaps influenced by changes that were taking place in neighbouring regions such as Greece. Sardinia was not affected by such depopulation and disruption and the Late Bronze Age saw the development of the multiple or complex *nuraghi* with strong defensive features, continuing through to the Iron Age.

In the Aegean region, it seems that many of the fortifications on the mainland and Cycladic islands were enlarged and strengthened, and the use of internal space was re-designed to allow greater storage and larger areas for production activities. Destruction, such as the great fire at Mycenae, continued to plague these sites and trade and communication was seriously disrupted at this time. The fate of the Bronze Age societies in the Aegean has already been discussed, and there remain many different theories on the likely causes and perpetrators of the decline which led into what has traditionally been termed the 'Dark Ages'.

DEFENSIVE EQUIPMENT

Throughout Europe, the panoply of arms and defensive equipment available to the Late Bronze Age warrior is greater than that of their Early Bronze Age predecessors. Warriors wore impressive objects of great beauty, including helmets, corselets and greaves. Such items were not always functional: the helmets of Viksø were certainly ceremonial rather than functional and the corselets (as well as several shield types) would have been of far more use in displays of power than for warfare itself, being too thin to afford much protection. Almost certainly, these gleaming bronzes would have copied more functional protective garb fashioned from organic materials; certainly we have examples of shields made both from wood and from leather. The famous Dendra bronze corselet found in the Aegean was heavy and strong and certainly *could* have been used – though it would have rendered the wearer almost immobile!

Defensive equipment is rarely found in the archaeological record of Spain, although this does not necessarily mean that there was no provision for defensive armour, but rather that these objects were most likely made from perishable materials which have not survived. The iconographic evidence suggests that helmets and shields were very much part of the warrior's panoply, although perhaps restricted to an elite section of the fighting force. This aside, the shift from archery to fighting at close quarters with swords and lances would have necessitated the use of shields and some form of body protection.

ICONOGRAPHY

As we have seen in the preceding chapters, artistic representations of warriors provide vital information for our understanding of Bronze Age warfare, in particular by illustrating the warriors' accoutrements. The famous Scandinavian carvings are hugely informative. Warriors are shown with shields, axes and swords. In addition, there are hints at the possible ceremonial nature of warrior status, with some figures wearing the great Viksø-style helmets and playing the curved ceremonial trumpets of the late period, the *lurs*.

In Late Bronze Age Spain, shields and wheeled vehicles are shown on grave stelae and there are a number of representations of helmets, shields, spears and swords which attest to an elaboration and diversification in the warrior's panoply of both defensive and offensive weapons. The symbolic or commemorative properties of these stelae and rock carvings can only be speculated, likewise the increase in hoarding weapons and votive offerings. Similar questions can be applied to the carvings found in Italy, especially the statue-stele as well as rock carvings such as those found at Monte Bego, as we see males roles being played out in the form of great hunters and warriors. The diversity of the iconographic evidence is a striking feature of the Italian Bronze Age, from the Sardinian bronze figurines to the anthropomorphic stelae and the rock art of the Italian Alps (pp. 107–11).

The iconographic evidence in the Aegean includes beautiful frescoes, stelae, seals and painted ceramic vessels and these suggest that the sword and spear were the main weapons of choice. Warriors were also provided with protective equipment: tower and figure-of-eight shields, padded leather armour and boars' tusk helmets are all portrayed.

In addition to the depictions of warriors and their weapons, other iconographic elements are vital to our understanding of the nature of Bronze Age fighting. Two recurring themes are boats and horses.

MOBILITY

Evidence for the use of boats for travel and transportation appears in a number of different forms, principally iconographic. From the depictions of boats in wall-paintings and as carvings on rocks and stelae, it is difficult to establish whether these reflect a common, everyday item, or something special and rare. The Scandinavian carvings show many boats, some of which have warriors on board holding axes and shields. It is possible that such figures are fighting one another. In the Late Bronze Age some of the burials were placed in graves that were lined with flat stones to give the grave the overall appearance of a boat. Perhaps the most dramatic artistic depiction of a war-band utilising a boat is the Roos Carr boat from Humberside (*see* p. 34; **Fig. 2.16**). The warriors were radiocarbon-dated to the Late Bronze Age/Early Iron Age and they have round shields and what may be clubs.

Wooden boats of Bronze Age date have been recovered from North Ferriby and Dover in England, and there is excavated evidence for the carrying of bronze cargoes across the English Channel by such vessels. Rivers were the 'super-highways' of much of the European mainland in the Bronze Age and it has been suggested that riverine routes are in part revealed by linking the rivers named 'Avon' in England. Goods were transported with ease along rivers throughout Europe, but just as trading parties could move along them so too could raiding parties hoping either to attack trading parties en route or perhaps to attack the fortified sites established along such riverine routes. This is not to say that bronzes and skeletal remains recovered from rivers were there as a result of fighting – bronzes were deliberately deposited in rivers and lakes as acts of propitiation in the Late Bronze Age. In addition, it may well be that bodies were excarnated in this period, the defleshed bones then being placed in watery locations, possibly as part of an overall water-cult.

However, there is ample other evidence for riverine raids. Although Iron Age in date, the a perfectly preserved boat from Hjortspring in Denmark was found with the equipment of a raiding party, including rectangular wooden shields and spears. This boat may have been deposited as an offering to the gods following the defeat of a raiding party. There seems no reason to suppose that such warfare was very different in the Late Bronze Age, especially as much of the weaponry types remained the same.

The situation regarding boats and raids appears to differ somewhat in the Aegean. There are depictions of galleys with warriors on board and there is a strong possibility that warfare actually took place at sea in this period. Furthermore, a number of Linear B tablets mention dangers coming from the sea. The importance of fighting ships may perhaps go some way to explain the lack of fortifications at the Minoan sites on Crete, as they might instead have maintained a strong fleet to deter attacks or to intercept enemies at sea. The numerous islands of the Aegean isolated somewhat from mainland Europe, might explain why sea warfare was not only possible but also important in this region. The depiction on a pottery vessel of a Greek warship fighting what seems to be an Etruscan vessel, combined with Greek and Latin writings describing sea battles around Italy, may also indicate that this more organised type of conflict also occurred in Italy.

If boats were important for transport along rivers and at sea, then horses enabled longer-distance movement on land. In the same manner as ships and boats, horse-borne transport not only enabled goods to be moved, but also provided mobility for attackers. Horse-trappings proliferate in the Late Bronze Age archaeological record, including objects destroyed by weaponry like the Melksham phalerae, and horse bones are also found. These beasts were not the large cavalry chargers of today but were more akin to the modern Shetland Pony. None the less they would enable the warrior to cover long distances to attack far-flung settlements. The cult wagon from Strettweg, datable to around Hallstatt C (the Late Bronze Age/Early Iron Age transition), shows a number of warriors on horseback, holding spears and protected by helmets and shields. Horses are also depicted in rock art in Iberia, Italy, northern and central Europe, and several appear to be pulling wagons or chariots, although such representations are difficult to define.

In the Aegean, one of the abiding images from epics such as Homer's *Iliad* is that of warriors clad in magnificent bronze armour and actually going to battle in chariots. Homer indicates that these were not used in a sort of chaotic charge but rather carried the warrior to the place of battle, where he would dismount to fight. Such chariots are also mentioned in the Linear B records. Although there seems to be no evidence for warriors of the Late Bronze Age on the European mainland using chariots in a formal battle, raiders may have ridden to the place of conflict before dismounting to fight. There also seems to be evidence for additional defence against raiders at fortified sites, with piles of stones just inside the defences, as at Pseira, that were probably hurled at the attackers.

Taken as a whole, the evidence suggests that warfare was certainly present among Bronze Age societies although the nature of the defences constructed, the types of weapons used and the tactics employed often varied between different regions. The degree to which warfare was part of everyday life is unclear, although weapons and warriors were familiar subjects in the art of the period and their status was celebrated within the sphere of funerary ritual and other ceremonial activities. It is thus possible to state with some confidence that warfare most certainly did take place in the European Bronze Age. Furthermore, with a close study of all the elements available through archaeology, one can begin to speculate on the possible causes of conflict and to discern changing styles of warfare as the period progresses.

CAUSES OF CONFLICT

The causes of Bronze Age warfare were doubtless many and varied, as is shown by a quick examination of the ethnographic literature. Warfare might be pursued in order to obtain slaves or to capture wives, for trade goods and the natural resources required for their production, to obtain prestige or power, for revenge and trophies, or for land and other motives. What broad conclusions can we draw about the reasons for fighting through the Bronze Age?

Almost certainly competition over tradable goods, so vital to the prestige goods network, was an important factor in the conflict of the Early Bronze Age. Amber, furs and suchlike were traded from the north of Europe, making their way along land passes and rivers to central Europe where they were exchanged for other goods such as salt and bronzes, or moved along to Italy and southern Europe. From the south, oils and wines moved up through central Europe in the same way, and thus central Europe played a pivotal role in the trading exchange network. In addition, the Wessex and Unetice Cultures traded prestige goods with nearby regions. That these trade-routes were important and possibly threatened in some way is shown by the establishment of fortified sites along the rivers and land passes that formed the route. Resources needed protection, and production even took place within sites provided with defences.

Such conflict over prestige goods was almost certainly present in the Late Bronze Age, alongside the new pressure for land. The later Bronze Age in many places sees the dividing up of the landscape with linear barriers and field systems and perhaps even the emergence of a tribal identity preceding the known Iron Age tribal groupings. As mentioned above, the rise of sedentism and increasing domestication of animals and plants may have added to these pressures. Land, food supplies and craft objects were of importance and therefore worth fighting over. The long-distance trade-routes from Scandinavia and northern Germany through central Europe and ultimately to Italy in the Late Bronze Age were vulnerable to attack. Much elite metalwork also passed from Hungary to northern Italy, with the trade-routes still utilising rivers – a fact borne out by the distribution of numerous object types, from tweezers and pins to spearheads and swords.

It has been suggested that slaves were also taken during raids of the Late Bronze Age. This may be reflected in the Germanic costume found in one of the Danish oak coffin burials, though it might equally represent the result of a marriage alliance or the transport of prestigious foreign clothing. Certainly there is no conclusive evidence for slave-taking.

SUMMARY

Although the regions of Europe have been treated as separate elements here, they did not exist in isolation and thus goods and ideas were able to move between them. This perhaps goes some way to explaining why distant regions shared so many similarities in forms of warfare. The Aegean had strong links not just with Europe but also with Egypt and it is possible that a papyrus from Amarna depicts Aegean warriors, wearing boar's tusk helmets, serving in Egypt during the reign of King Akhenaten (known as the 'heretic King' and father of Tutankhamen). In addition, some of the region's defensive fortifications have arrow slots, even though there appears to be relatively little evidence for archery compared with the rest of Europe. This may well indicate the existence of links with mainland Europe.

Objects and cultural phenomena, such as the Beaker Culture and the Atlantic distribution of Carp's Tongue swords, are shared throughout mainland Europe. Furthermore, bronze objects have distinct location patterns along rivers in different regions. The rites of burial, although not universal, seem to be similar over large tracts of Europe, from the inhumations of the Tumulus Culture to the cremations of the Urnfield Period. Trade routes (and chronological changes to them) are visible from southern Europe to the north and it has been suggested in some quarters that mercenary warriors may even have moved between these regions.

Styles of warfare certainly changed through time in the Bronze Age. At its dawn archery was dominant and warfare took place at longer range. Bladed weapons then grew in importance and the dagger of the Early Bronze Age was replaced by the rapiers – a weapon of the champion as it required training in its use. Spears too were introduced towards the end of the Early Bronze Age, perhaps replacing arrows as the leading projectile-based weapon and prestige object (though there is a substantial body of evidence that archery was still used). The rapier was then replaced by the leaf-shaped sword and this weapon, alongside spears and armour, was the weapon of choice for the warriors of raiding war-bands in the Late Bronze Age. These groups made use of boats and horses for movement through the landscape and fought at close range. In the Aegean horses may have been used to pull chariots to carry the warrior to the point of conflict and it seems likely that ships played a hugely significant role, either in fighting at sea or in piracy.

Much of the evidence from Europe is open to many different interpretations, and it is difficult to discern whether it represents actual warfare or a more symbolic, ceremonial entity. The construction of fortifications and the presence of bronze armour and rock art could all have been undertaken for the prestige of individuals who were not actively engaged in fighting, or might illustrate mythological engagements rather than being a direct representation of fighting. The social and symbolic use of weapons, of objects associated with warriors and of defensive structures meant that readiness for war was as important as the actual fighting itself. Across much of Europe, the increasing ritual and symbolic significance of weapons and objects associated with warriors may suggest that the brutal act of fighting was being replaced by more symbolic gestures: competitive feasting, exchange of gifts, alliance-building and ritual duelling. In other words, fighting was perceived as an 'event' interrupting an otherwise peaceful way of life, rather than as an ever-present part of everyday life.

In essence, this book has tried to challenge, and in some cases reinforce or disprove, some of the general perceptions of prehistoric warfare. All of the chapters have been able to show clear occurrences of the actuality of warfare, and also its forms and perhaps its causes, indicating that Bronze Age warfare was not simply a ceremonial activity – it was a very real and deadly phenomenon. In many ways, the evidence seems to suggest that warriors became less concerned with the actual physical aspects of fighting and more preoccupied with gaining access to bronze weapons and other status objects, and with their conspicuous consumption in ceremonial activities and funerary rituals. At the same time, certainly towards the end of the Bronze Age, the 'ordinary' warrior has become less evident in the archaeological record (especially the burial record) and therefore the interpretation of the evidence in the later period may reflect only one aspect of warfare – the elite aspect. The evidence cited in the preceding chapters has highlighted the complexities and pitfalls of assessing large bodies of data from a range of disciplines (excavation, survey, skeletal analysis, artefact studies, analysis of funerary remains) across a wide geographical area. As we have shown, some of the evidence is ambiguous and can be interpreted in a number of different ways but it is only through studying a broad base of cultural groups that we can begin to see patterns emerging. We do not presume to have had the last word on the subject and there is much research that needs to be done in the future but, if nothing else, we hope this discussion has helped to promote a greater interest in the nature of prehistoric warfare, and perhaps encouraged at least some readers to question their preconceptions of what warfare and its participants were like in the Bronze Age.

GLOSSARY

Acropolis:	A citadel or fortified area built on high ground.
Bastion:	A defensive structure, usually semi-circular or rectangular, projecting from a fortification wall.
Beaker:	Ceramic vessel found throughout Europe in the Late Neolithic and Early Bronze Age. Beakers were part of a burial package within round barrows alongside flint arrowheads, bronze daggers and stone wristguards.
Carp's Tongue [sword]:	A Late Bronze Age sword type with an Atlantic distribution. The blade of this sword variant tapers to a narrower extended tip with parallel sides to combine the slashing and stabbing attributes of earlier weapon types.
Chapes:	A metal mounting on the tip of a sword scabbard, sometimes hooked to enabled quick removal of a sword from its sheath by a mounted warrior.
Cinerary urn:	An urn for holding a person's ashes after cremation.
Cist [burial]:	A burial within a grave, often square in shape and with edges defined by upright slabs of stone.
Corselet:	A piece of armour covering the trunk of the body.
Cuirass:	Body armour comprising both back and breastplate. Bronze examples have been recovered from the archaeological record, probably with parallels made from organic materials for use in combat.
Dirk:	A short stabbing bladed weapon, much like a dagger.
Eneolithic/Chalcolithic:	Copper Age.
Excarnation:	The exposing of a dead body in the open air, until it has become defleshed, as part of a burial rite.
Ferrule:	a metal lug/cap on the end of a tool or weapon.
Greaves:	Protective armour for the lower leg of the warrior. Bronze examples from the Late Bronze Age have been found in Europe.
Halberd:	A bronze weapon with a flat, triangular blade mounted at a right angle to the haft.
Hilt:	The handle section of a bladed weapon.
Latial:	Early Iron Age culture of Central Italy, south of Rome, with some similarities to the Urnfield Culture north of the Alps.

Lurs:	Bronze trumpets found in Scandinavia. They are composed of long curving tubes of bronze which were cast in separate sections and then joined.
Motilla:	A form of fortified site from the region of La Mancha in Spain.
Nuraghe (pl. Nuraghi):	Sardinian stone towers of Bronze to Iron Age date; hence the name of the Nuragic civilisation of which they are such a feature.
Oppida:	Fortified towns, in Caesar's terms, with industrial as well as habitation elements.
Osteology:	The study of the structure and function of bones.
Palafitta (pl. palafitte):	Lakeside settlements erected on pilings in northern Italy, dating to the Neolithic and Bronze Age. The waterlogged deposits yield well-preserved organic material.
Palisade:	A timber fence barrier.
Palmela point:	A leaf-shaped copper blade probably hafted to a long wooden shaft and used as a javelin (Spain).
Palstaves:	A bronze tool, similar in form to an axe, with the blade divided from the haft of the weapon by a ridge.
Panoply:	The complete collection of defensive and offensive arms of the warrior.
Parapet:	A protective embankment within a fortification, constructed from stone, timber or earth.
Pilum:	The pilum was the standard throwing spear of the Roman army. It had a small tip at the end of a long, slender neck. The iron projectile shaft was fitted into a solid wooden haft. The pilum employed the principle of encumbrance: once embedded in an opponent's shield, the weight of the wooden shaft would have caused the spearhead to bend over, thus rendering the shield useless.
Rampart:	A defensive barrier. These varied in form in the Bronze Age from simple earthen constructions to elaborate timber and stone box-ramparts.
Rapier:	A slender, tapering weapon with a sharp point, used in a thrusting motion. The rapier was superseded by the sword.
Scabbard:	A sheath for the blade of a sword.
Sedentism:	A lifestyle involving a degree of fixed status within the landscape as opposed to the greater movement of a nomadic lifestyle.
Shield-former:	A wooden shield mould into which a piece of leather was beaten to form the shield.
Stela (pl. stelae):	An upright stone or monolith which has been carved.
Terramara (pl. terremare):	Bronze Age settlements in the Po valley distinguished by deep deposits of domestic rubbish in a dark earth from which the name is derived.
Trivallate:	A defensive construction of three ramparts.

Urnfield: A period of Late Bronze Age Europe named after the method of disposing the dead as groups of cremations in ceramic vessels within large open cemeteries.

Villanovan: Early Iron Age culture located in central Italy, north of Rome, and in parts of the Po valley and Campania. The culture, which shows some similarities to the Urnfield Culture north of the Alps in its cemeteries and grave-goods, developed into the Etruscan civilisation.

Votive offering: Objects deposited in a manner that is suggestive of a religious ritual; this can take the form of a hoard or a single object, often placed in lakes and rivers.

Wristguards: Protective objects for the wrist of the archer. They were composed in the Early Bronze Age of thin sub-rectangular, flat fragments of stone, all of which have perforations to allow for hide or sinew ties. Wristguards were part of the burial package in the Beaker Period.

BIBLIOGRAPHY

Acheson, P.E. 1999. 'The Role of Force in the Development of Early Mycenaean Polities', in R. Laffineur (ed.). *Aegaeum 19: Polemos, Le Contexte Guerrier en Egée a l'Age du Bronze* (Univ. de Liège), pp. 97–104

Acosta, P. 1968. *La Pintura Rupestre Esquematica en España* (Salamanca)

Almagro Gorbea, M. 1973 'Cascos del bronce final en la peninsula Iberica', *Trabajos de Prehistoria* 30: 349–361

Ambrosi, A. 1988. *Statue-stele lunigianesi* (Sagep)

Anati, E. 1961. *Camonica Valley* (Alfred A. Knopf)

Anati, E. 1972. *I pugnali nell'arte rupestre e nelle statue-stele dell'Italia settentrionale* (del Centro)

Anati, E. 1981. *Le statue-stele di Lunigiana* (Jaca Book)

Arnott, R. 'War wounds and their treatment in the Aegean Bronze Age', in R. Laffineur (ed.). *Aegaeum 19: Polemos, Le Contexte Guerrier en Egée a l'Age du Bronze* (Univ. de Liège), pp. 499–506

Bartlett, J.E. & Hawkes, C.F.C. 1965. 'A Barbed Bronze Spearhead from North Ferriby, Yorkshire, England', *Proceedings of the Prehistoric Society* 31: 370–3

Beltrán, A. 1982. *Rock Art of the Spanish Levant* (Cambridge University Press)

Beltrán, A. *et al.* 1986. *El Arte Rupestre* (Historia de Cartagena II, Murcia)

Bennike, P. 1985. *Palaeopathology of Danish Skeletons: a comparative study of Demography, Disease and Injury* (Copenhagen Akademisk Forlag)

Bianco Peroni, V. 1970. *Die Schwerter in Italien/Le spade nell'Italia continentale* (Prähistorische Bronzefunde IV, 1)

Bianco Peroni, V. 1994. *I pugnali nell'Italia continentale* (Prähistorische Bronzefunde VI, 10)

Bietti Sestieri, A.M. 1993. *The Iron Age Community of Osteria dell'Osa* (Cambridge University Press)

Bóna, I. 1975. 'Die Mittlere Bronzezeit Ungarns und ihre südöstlichen beziehungen', *Archaeologia Hungarica* 49

Bonghi Jovino, M. (ed.). 1986. *Gli Etruschi di Tarquinia* (Panini)

Boos, A. 1999. 'The Chieftain's Grave of Hagenau and Related Warrior Graves', in K. Demakopoulou *et al.* (eds), *Gods and Heroes of the European Bronze Age* (Thames & Hudson), pp. 106–7

Bradley, R. 1997. *Rock Art in the Prehistory of Atlantic Europe* (Routledge)

Bradley, R. 1998. *The Passage of Arms: an archaeological analysis of prehistoric hoards and votive deposits* (Oxbow)

Bradley, R. & Ellison, A. 1975. *Rams Hill: A Bronze Age Defended Settlement and its Landscape* (British Archaeological Reports British Series 19)

Bradley, R., Chambers, R.A. & Halpin, C.E. (eds). 1984. *Barrow Hills, Radley 1983–4. Excavations: an Interim Report* (Oxford Archaeology Unit)

Branigan, K. 1999. 'The Nature of Warfare in the Southern Aegean during the Third Millennium B.C.', in R. Laffineur (ed.), *Aegaeum 19: Polemos, Le Contexte Guerrier en Egée a l'Age du Bronze* (Univ. de Liège) pp. 87–96

Breitinger, E. 1976. 'Das Kalvarium unter dem späturnenfelderzeitlichen Wall von Stillfried an der March', *Forschungen in Stillfried Band* 2: 86–100

Bridgford, S. 1997. 'Mightier than the Pen? An edgewise look at Irish Bronze Age swords', in J. Carman (ed.), *Material Harm: archaeological studies of war and violence* (Cruithne) pp. 95–115

Bukowski, Z. 1962. 'Fortified Settlements of Lusatian Culture in Great Poland and Kujawy in the light of research carried out in the years 1945–1960', *Archaeologia Polona* 4

Campillo, D. 1995. 'Agressivitat i violéncia a les societats prehistóriques i primitives', *Limes. Revista D'Arqueologia*: 4–16

Campillo, D., Mercadal, O. & Blanch, R. 1993. 'A mortal wound caused by a flint arrowhead in individual MF–18 of the neolithic period exhumed at Sant Quirze del Valles', *International Journal of Osteoarchaeology* (3): 145–50

Carman, J. (ed.). 1997. *Material Harm: archaeological studies of war and violence* (Cruithne)

Carman, J. & Harding, A.F. (eds). 1999. *Ancient Warfare* (Suttons)

Castleden, R. 1993. *Minoans. Life in Bronze Age Crete* (Routledge)

Castro Martínez, P.V., Lull, V. & Micó, R. 1996. *Cronología de la Prehistoria Reciente de la Península Ibérica y Baleares (c. 2800–900 Cal ANE)* (British Archaeological Reports International Series 652)

Chapman, R. 1990. *Emerging Complexity: The later prehistory of south-east Spain, Iberia and the west Mediterranean* (Cambridge University Press)

Cocchi Genick, D. (ed.). 1996. *L'antica età del bronzo in Italia* (Octavo)

Coles, J.M. 1962. 'European Bronze Age Shields', *Proceedings of the Prehistoric Society* 28: 156–90

Coles, J.M. 1990. *Images of the Past: a guide to the rock carvings and other ancient monuments of Northern Bohuslän* (Hällristningsmuseet)

Coles, J.M. & Harding, A.F. 1979. *The Bronze Age in Europe* (Methuen)

Cunliffe, B.W. (ed.). 1987. *Origins: The Roots of European Civilisation* (BBC)

Cunliffe, B.W. (ed.). 1994. *The Oxford Illustrated Prehistory of Europe* (Oxford University Press)

Demakopoulou, K. 1999a. 'Aegean Palaces', in K. Demakopoulou *et al.* (eds) *Gods and Heroes of the European Bronze Age* (Thames & Hudson), pp. 66–9

Demakopoulou, K. 1999b. 'Funeral Architecture and Burial Customs in the Aegean', in K. Demakopoulou *et al.* (eds), *Gods and Heroes of the European Bronze Age* (Thames & Hudson) pp. 98–101

Demakopoulou, K., Eluère, C., Jensen, J., Jockenhövel, A. & Mohen, J.-P. (eds). 1999. *Gods and Heroes of the European Bronze Age* (Thames & Hudson)

Demakopoulou, K. & Divari-Valakou, N. 1999. 'The Fortifications of the Mycenaean Acropolis of Midea', in R. Laffineur (ed.), *Aegaeum 19: Polemos, Le Contexte Guerrier en Egée a l'Age du Bronze* (Univ. de Liège) pp. 205–18

Dickinson, O. 1994. *The Aegean Bronze Age* (Cambridge University Press)

Drews, R. 1993. *The End of the Bronze Age. Changes in warfare and the catastrophe ca. 1200 BC* (Princeton University Press3)

Driessen, J. 1999. 'The Archaeology of Aegean Warfare', in R. Laffineur (ed.), *Aegaeum 19: Polemos, Le Contexte Guerrier en Egée a l'Age du Bronze* (Univ. de Liège), pp. 11–20

Egg, M. 1990. *Antike Helme: Katalog zur Ausstellung des Landes Rheinland-Pfalz in Verbindung mit der Stiftung Preussischer Kulturbesitz Berlin* (Römisch-Germanischen Zentralmuseums)

Etxeberria, F., Herrasti, L. & Vegas, J.I. 1995. 'Arrow wounds during prehistory in the Iberian Peninsula with regard to San Juan ante Portam Latinam', in *Proceedings of the IXth European meeting of the Paleopathology Association* (Barcelona, 1–4 September 1992) (Museu D'Arqueologia de Catalunya, Barcelona), pp. 141–5.

Etxeberria, F. & Vegas, J.I. 1988a. 'Heridas por flecha durante la prehistoria en la península Ibérica', *Munibe (Antropologia–Arkeologia) Suplemento No. 8*: 129–36

Etxeberria, F. & Vegas, J.I. 1988b. 'Agresividad social o guerra? durante el Neo-enelítico en la cuenca media del Valle Ebro, a propósito de San Juan Ante Portam Latinam (Rioja alavesa)', *Munibe (Antropología y Arqueología) Supplemento No. 6*: 105–12

Evans, J.G. 1984. 'Stonehenge: the Environment in the Late Neolithic and Early Bronze Age and a Beaker Burial', *Wiltshire Archaeological Magazine* 78: 7–30

Fernández Manzano, J. & Montero Ruiz, I. 1997. 'Las armas durante el calcolítico y la edad del bronce', in *La Guerra en la Antiguedad. Una aprozimación al origen de los ejércitos en Hispania* (Ministerio de Defensa: Madrid) pp. 109–22

Feustel, R. 1958. *Bronzezeitliche Hügelgräberkultur in Gebeit von Schwarza (Sudthüringen)* (Herman Böhlaus Nachfolger)

Fleming, A. 1988. *The Dartmoor Reaves* (Batsford)

Fröhlich, S. 1983. *Studien zur Mittleren Bronzezeit zwischen Thüringer Wald und Altmark, Leipziger Tieflandsbucht und Oker* (Braunschweigischen Landesmuseums)

Gallay, A. 1978. 'Stèles néolithiques et problématique archaeologique', *Archives Suisses d'Anthropologie Générale* 42 (2): 75–103

Gilman, A. & Thornes, J.B. 1985. *Land-use and Prehistory in South-east Spain* (George Allen & Unwin)

Gimbutas, M. 1965. *Bronze Age Cultures in Central and Eastern Europe* (Mouton)

Glob, P.V. 1974. *The Mound People: Danish Bronze Age Man Preserved* (Faber & Faber)

Halstead, P. 1994. 'The North–South Divide: Regional Paths to Complexity in Prehistoric Greece', in C. Mathers & S. Stoddart (eds), *Development and Decline in the Mediterranean Bronze Age* (Sheffield Academic Press), pp. 195–219

Harding, A.F. 1994. 'Reformation in Barbarian Europe, 1300–600 BC', in B.W. Cunliffe (ed.), *The Oxford Illustrated Prehistory of Europe* (Oxford University Press), pp. 304–35

Harding, A.F. 1999. 'Warfare: a Defining Characteristic of Bronze Age Europe?', in J. Carman & A. Harding (eds), *Ancient Warfare* (Sutton), pp. 157–73

Harding, A.F. 2000. *European Societies in the Bronze Age* (Cambridge University Press)

Härke, H. 1979. *Settlement Types and Settlement Patterns in the West Hallstatt Province: an Evaluation from Excavated Sites Europe* (British Archaeological Reports International Series 57)

Harrison, R.J. 1994. 'The Bronze Age in Northern and Northeastern Spain 2000–800 BC', in C. Mathers & S. Stoddart (eds), *Development and Decline in the Mediterranean Bronze Age* (Sheffield Archaeological Monographs 8, J.R. Collis), pp. 73–98

Hencken, H. 1971. *The Earliest European Helmets: Bronze Age and Early Iron Age* (Peabody Museum, Harvard University)

Hrala, J., Sedláek, Z. & Vávra, M. 1992. 'Velim: a hilltop site of the Middle Bronze Age in Bohemia', *Památky Archeologické* 83: 288–308

Janssens, P.A. 1970. *Palaeopathology: Diseases and Injuries of Prehistory* (Baker)

Jockenhövel, A. 1975. 'Zu befestigten siedlungen der Urnenfelderzeit aus süddeutschland', *Fundberichte aud Hessen* 14: 19–62

Jockenhövel, A. 1999. 'Bronze Age Fortresses in Europe: Territorial Security', in K. Demakopoulou *et al.* (eds), *Gods and Heroes of the European Bronze Age* (Thames & Hudson), pp. 71–2

Jorge, S. Oliveira. 1999a. 'Bronze Age Settlements and Territories on the Iberian Peninsula: New considerations', in K. Demakopoulou *et al.* (eds), *Gods and Heroes of the European Bronze Age* (Thames & Hudson), pp. 60–4

Jorge, S. Oliveira. 1999b. 'Bronze Age Stelai and Menhirs of the Iberian Peninsula: Discourses of power', in K. Demakopoulou *et al.* (eds), *Gods and Heroes of the European Bronze Age* (Thames & Hudson), pp. 114–22

Karoušková-Soper, V. 1983. *Castellieri of the Venezia Giulia, North-eastern Italy (2nd–1st Millennium BC)* (British Archaeological Reports International Series 192)

Knight, R.W., Browne, C. & Grinsell, L.V. 1972. 'Prehistoric skeletons from Tormarton', *Transactions of the Bristol and Gloucester Archaeological Society* 91: 14–17

Kovács, T. 1999. 'Tell Settlements in the Danube Region', in K. Demakopoulou *et al.* (eds), *Gods and Heroes of the European Bronze Age* (Thames & Hudson), p. 65

Larsson, T. & Lundmark, H. (eds). 1989. *Approaches to Swedish Prehistory : A Spectrum of Problems and Perspectives in Contemporary Research* (British Archaeological Reports International Series 500)

Leighton, R. 1999. *Sicily before History* (Duckworth)

Manning, S. 1994. 'The Emergence of Divergence: Development and Decline on Bronze Age Crete and the Cyclades', in C. Mathers & S. Stoddart (eds), *Development and Decline in the Mediterranean Bronze Age* (Sheffield Academic Press), pp. 221–70

Manning, S. 1995. *The Absolute Chronology of the Aegean Bronze Age* (Sheffield Academic Press)

Martín, A. 1991. 'The Bronze Age of La Mancha', *Antiquity* 67: 23–45

Martin, D.L. & Frayer, D.W. (eds). 1997. *Troubled times: violence and warfare in the past* (Gordon Breach)

Michaels, J.W. & Webster, G.S. (eds). 1987. *Studies in Nuragic archaeology* (British Archaeological Reports International Series 373)

Monks, S.J. 1997. 'Conflict and competition in Spanish prehistory: the role of warfare in societal development from the late fourth to third millennium BC', *Journal of Mediterranean Archaeology* 10 (1): 3–32

Monks, S.J. 1998. 'The role of conflict and competition in the development of prehistoric west Mediterranean societies from the late 4th to early 2nd millennium BC', Unpublished PhD thesis, University of Reading

Monks, S.J. 1999. 'Patterns of Warfare and Settlement in Southeast Spain', *Journal of Iberian Archaeology* 1: 127–71

Morgan, L. 1988. *The Miniature Wall Paintings of Thera* (Cambridge University Press)

Müller-Karpe, H. 1959. *Beiträge zur Chronologie der Urnenfelderzeit nördlich und südlich der Alpen* (de Gruyter)

Musson, C.R. 1991. *The Breiddin Hillfort: A later Prehistoric Settlement in the Welsh Marches* (CBA Research Report 76)

Needham, S. 1979. 'Two Recent British Shield Finds and their Continental Parallels', *Proceedings of the Prehistoric Society* 45: 111–34

Nordbladh, J. 1989. 'Armour and fighting in the south Scandinavian Bronze Age, especially in view of rock art representations', in T.B. Larsson & H. Lundmark (eds), *Approaches to Swedish Prehistory: A Spectrum of Problems and Perspectives in Contemporary Research* (British Archaeological Reports International Series 500), pp. 323–33

Oosterbeek, L. 1997. 'War in the Chalcolithic? The meaning of the West Mediterranean hillforts', in J. Carman (ed.), *Material Harm: archaeological studies of war and violence* (Cruithne Press), pp. 116–32

Osgood, R.H. 1998. *Warfare in the Late Bronze Age of North Europe* (British Archaeological Reports International Series 694)

Palaima, T. 1999. 'Mycenaean Militarism from a Textual Perspective', in R. Laffineur (ed.), *Aegaeum 19: Polemos, Le Contexte Guerrier en Egée a l'Age du Bronze* (Univ. de Liège), pp. 367–80

Pare, C.F.E. 1999. 'Wagon Graves of the Late Bronze Age', in K. Demakopoulou *et al.* (eds), *Gods and Heroes of the European Bronze Age* (Thames and Hudson), pp. 125–6

Parker Pearson, M. 1993. *The English Heritage Book of Bronze Age Britain* (English Heritage)

Patay, P. 1968. 'Urnenfelderzeitliche Bronzeschilde im Karpatenbecken', *Germania* 46: 241–8

Peatfield, A.D. 1999. 'The Paradox of Violence: Weaponry and Martial Art in Minoan Crete', in R. Laffineur (ed.) *Aegaeum 19: Polemos, Le Contexte Guerrier en Egée a l'Age du Bronze* (Univ. de Liège), pp. 67–74

Peroni, R. 1994. *Introduzione alla protostoria italiana* (Laterza)

Piggott, S. 1965. *Ancient Europe* (Edinburgh University Press)

Plesl, E. 1961. *Lužická kultura ve severozápadnich echách* (Eskoslovenské Akademie Vd)

Preziosi, D. & Hitchcock, L.A. 1999. *Aegean Art and Architecture* (Oxford University Press)

Priuli, A. 1985. *Incisioni rupestri della Valcamonica* (Torino)

Priuli, A. 1988. *Incisioni rupestri di Monte Bego* (Torino)

Randsborg, K. 1995. *Hjortspring: Warfare and Sacrifice in Early Europe* (Aarhus University Press)

Renfrew, C. 1972. *The Emergence of Civilisation: The Cyclades and the Aegean in the Third Millennium BC* (Methuen)

Richards, J. 1991. *The English Heritage Book of Stonehenge* (English Heritage)

Robb, J. 1994. 'Gender contradictions, moral coalitions, and inequality in prehistoric Italy', *Journal of European Archaeology* 2.1, pp. 20–49

Robb, J. 1997a. 'Violence and Gender in Early Italy', in D.L. Martin & D.W. Frayer (eds), *Troubled times: violence and warfare in the past* (Gordon Breach), pp. 111–44

Robb, J. 1997b. 'Female beauty and male violence in early Italian society', in A.O. Koloski-Ostrovo & C.L. Lyons (eds), *Naked truths: women, sexuality and gender in classical art and archaeology* (Routledge)

Ruíz-Gálvez Priego, M. 1997. 'The West of Iberia: Meeting Point between the Mediterranean and the Atlantic at the End of the Bronze Age', in M.S. Balmuth, A. Gilman & L. Prados-Torreira (eds), *Encounters and Transformations: The Archaeology of Iberia in Transition* (Sheffield Academic Press) pp. 95–120

Santillo Frizell, B. (ed.). 1991. *Arte militare e architettura nuragica (Nuragic architecture in its military, territorial and socio-economic context)*, Conference proceedings: Skrifter utvigna av Svenska Institutet i Rom, 4, xlviii

Sherratt, A. 1993. 'What would a Bronze Age world system look like? Relations between Temperate Europe and the Mediterranean in later Prehistory', *Journal of European Archaeology* 1, 2: 1–57

Sherratt, A.G. 1987. 'Warriors and Traders: Bronze Age Chiefdoms in Central Europe', in B.W. Cunliffe (ed.), *Origins: The Roots of European Civilisation* (BBC)

Sherratt, A.G. 1994. 'The Emergence of Élites: Earlier Bronze Age Europe, 2500–1300 BC', in B.W. Cunliffe (ed.), *The Oxford Illustrated Prehistory of Europe* (Oxford University Press), pp. 244–76

Spindler, K. 1994. *The Man in the Ice* (Weidenfeld & Nicolson)

Stary, P. 1991. 'Arms and armour of the Nuragic warrior-statuettes' in B. Santillo Frizell (ed.), *Arte militare e architettura nuragica (Nuragic architecture in its military, territorial and socio-economic context)*, pp. 119–42. Conference proceedings: Skrifter utvigna av Svenska Institutet i Rom, 4, xlviii

Stead, I.M. 1991. *Iron Age Cemeteries in East Yorkshire* (English Heritage Archaeological Report 22)

Tihelka, K. 1969. 'Velatice Culture Burials at Bluina', *Fontes Archeologici Pragenses* 13

Točík, A. & Paulík, J. 1960. 'Výskum Mohyly v ake v Rokoch 1950–1', *Slovenská Archeológia* 8 (1): 59–124

Trump, D. 1966. *Central and Southern Italy before Rome* (Thames & Hudson)

Trump, D.H. 1992. 'Militarism in Nuragic Sardinia', in R.H. Tykot & T.K. Andrews (eds), *Sardinia in the Mediterranean: a footprint in the sea* (Sheffield Academic Press), pp. 198–203

Tykot, R.H. & Andrews, T.K. (eds), *Sardinia in the Mediterranean: a footprint in the sea* (Sheffield Academic Press)

Vaquerizo Gil, D. 1989. '"Estelas de Guerreros" en la protohistoria peninsular', *Revista de Arqueologia* 99: 29–38

von Brunn, W.A. 1959. *Bronzezeitliche Hortfunde, Teil I Die Hortfunde der frühen Bronzezeit aus Sachsen-Anhalt, Sachsen, Thüringer* (Akad. Verlag)

von Merhart, G. 1958. 'Geschnürte Schienen', in *Bericht der Römisch-Germanischen Komission* 37–8: 91–147

Webster, G.S. 1996. *A Prehistory of Sardinia 2300–500 BC* (Sheffield Academic Press)

Wedde, M. 1999. 'War at Sea: the Mycenaean and Early Iron Age Oared Galley', in R. Laffineur (ed.), *Aegaeum 19: Polemos, Le Contexte Guerrier en Egée a l'Age du Bronze* (Univ. de Liège) pp. 465–78

INDEX